PROPERTY/ CASUALTY INSURANCE

A Basic Guide

PROPERTY/ CASUALTY INSURANCE

A Basic Guide

For Adjusters, Underwriters, Agents, Brokers,
Attorneys, Entrepreneurs, and Business Managers

Ernest H. Gore

For Elizabeth — my wife, my partner, my best friend.

Table of Contents

PART I – INSURANCE IN GENERAL

PART II – SPECIFIC COVERAGES

PART III - APPENDIX

Acknowledgements

I could not have completed this manual without the physical and emotional help I received from four good friends.

My thanks go out to my wife, Elizabeth, for her on-going encouragement, as well as her assistance in editing and offering useful suggestions. The same is true of three colleagues with whom I have had the pleasure of working over the years: Mike Conroy, Eric Jones, and Don Prue.

Each of these trusted friends had the opportunity to read part or all of the unfinished manuscript, and to offer specific suggestions and ideas.

The end product reflects not only my efforts, but theirs as well.

About the Author

M r. Gore has spent more than 40 years working in the insurance industry. He has been a consultant to insurance companies, to insured and self-insured business entities, and to private and governmental agencies throughout the United States and Britain.

Before becoming a consultant, he held Senior/Executive Officer positions with three international insurance carriers.

His background includes experience teaching in The Extension Program of the Business School at the University of California at Los Angeles (UCLA), as a Guest Lecturer for several years at The Marshall School for Graduate Studies in Business Administration at The University of Southern California (USC), and as an instructor at The Adjuster Academy in Los Angeles.

He has devised, established and conducted training programs for several insurance entities.

Mr. Gore has had several articles published in industry trade journals addressing various insurance related subjects:

> "The Baby & The Bath Water; Be Careful What You Throw Out If You Decide It's Time To Change Your TPA."; The Self Insurer magazine; published by The Self Insurance Institute of America (SIIA); February, 2000 edition.

> "The Chess Game of TPA Contract Negotiations"; Risk Management magazine; published by Risk and Insurance Management Society (RIMS); June, 2000 ed.

> "Auditing Your TPA Claim Files"; Risk Management magazine; published by Risk and Insurance Management Society (RIMS); January, 2001 edition.

> "Foundation, Foundation, Foundation. Negotiating the TPA Contract." The Self Insurer magazine; published by The Self Insurance Institute of America (SIIA); March 2006 Edition;

> "Qualifying an Expert Witness"; Risk Management magazine; published by Risk and Insurance Management Society (RIMS); September, 2006 edition.

He has been designated as an expert witness on dozens of lawsuits involving matters of insurance coverage, and has testified numerous times on these issues in Federal Court cases, and in numerous State Courts throughout the United States.

Preface

This book was written as a general overview of the world of property and casualty insurance. The text is presented in such a way as to allow the general reader to learn about, and understand, some of the historical, technical, and legal nuances of this complex industry. It is not meant as a scholarly tome covering all the various intricacies of this ever-evolving segment of our business landscape. Entire libraries exist for that purpose. It is, however, the author's hope and opinion that the serious student of this subject will find the information contained herein to be helpful, and of some use in charting a course to the proper and appropriate areas for specific questions or solutions.

Much of our daily lives is influenced – one way or another – by insurance. If we have the correct policies to protect our personal and/or business assets, but never suffer a loss, we have paid (in the form of premiums) for the peace of mind, which comes from feeling protected.

If we sustain a loss that is covered by one of our policies, we can feel grateful that some other entity will pay, or share, the economic impact of such a situation.

If we failed to purchase the appropriate insurance, a loss may be borne by us without financial assistance or aid from an insurer, and we will bear most or all of the loss ourselves.

In each of these situations, insurance will affect us economically, and perhaps psychologically. Since the industry touches upon all manner of things with which many people never receive specific training — contracts, building construction, civil ordinances, law, and medicine, to name a few — it will be useful to recognize and become familiar with the jargon and terms which are ordinary and customary in the industry.

The chapters of this book will acquaint the reader with the general types of insurance companies, the various job functions within the companies, some ancillary aspects related to this industry, and the general terms and conditions of the more predominant types of property and casualty insurance policies. At the end of the book is an extensive Glossary containing hundreds of insurance industry terms, as well as legal terms generally related to the world of insurance, with easy to understand definitions.

The material contained in the manual is not intended to be considered as legal advice. I am not an attorney and therefore not allowed to render such advice. The comments related to legal principles and matters of law are the opinions and observations of myself as a layman. In the event a legal question arises, the reader is encouraged to seek professional assistance from a licensed attorney who is admitted to the Bar in the specific jurisdiction in which the legal question or situation has arisen.

I hope you will find the book informative, helpful, and interesting.

Ernest H. Gore

PART I

Insurance in General

CHAPTER ONE

A Brief History of Insurance

I n the 1600s, the military sea power of the British Empire (having no peer at the time) spawned a civilian industry that opened up mercantile markets around the world. This new industry was commercial shipping.

Owners of ocean going vessels found willing manufacturers who were interested in supplying their goods to retailers and consumers in Europe, North America, and the Caribbean Islands. The perils experienced at sea were considerable, and much more fearsome than transporting goods by land, where safe havens from weather, bandits, and even negligent handling could be more easily foreseen and possibly avoided.

As a result, the owners of the goods, and the ship owners, sought ways to minimize the exposure to these risks. It did not take long for this relatively small and close knit group to realize many ships arrived at their destination safe, on time, and without incident. Others, however, never arrived, or arrived with lost, missing, or damaged cargo. The owners whose ship and/or goods arrived safe thanked their good fortune, and waited for the next venture. Those who were less fortunate and suffered a loss of their property, either cursed their misfortune and attempted to recoup the loss on the next shipment, or were unable to continue in business.

Some of the more farsighted businessmen began to realize that if they could average out their losses, they could reduce the potential for catastrophe. If they could collectively share their losses when they occurred, then individually they could minimize the impact of a catastrophe that might otherwise drive them to bankruptcy.

This concept of attempting to share the risk and the rewards by joining forces was not new or unique to this group of Englishmen. Hundreds of years before this, Chinese boatmen sailing their vessels along the Yangtze River in China, as well as Venetians sailing the Mediterranean, had learned that they could similarly group together to minimize their losses, and thus increase their riches. The practice was greatly refined in London as the industry grew and flourished.

Near the end of the 17th Century, a man named Edward Lloyd was the owner of a London coffee shop on Tower Street, near the London docks. Each day, Mr. Lloyd would post the latest shipping information on his coffee shop bulletin board. This practice began to attract both ship owners and merchants wishing to engage ships to transport their wares to foreign markets.

At the Lloyd's Coffee House, participants could meet and hire ships to move their goods to the new markets around the world, or find merchants seeking a sturdy ship for hire. They could also discuss whether they might find one or more fellow shippers who would be interested in sharing the potential for loss, and the potential for profit.

In 1771, a group of those having become involved in this new and growing enterprise of trying to balance the risk of sea transportation, moved from the Lloyd's Coffee House and took up commercial residence in the London financial district where a more conventional business atmosphere could be established. They did, however, retain their group identity as Lloyd's of London.

This prospering new venture of the shipping industry soon gave rise to other enterprising individuals who themselves had no ship to sail, nor goods to transport. They, nevertheless, were quite willing to help the owners defray part of their risk, in exchange for a part of their profits. These individuals were willing to underwrite the ventures and were, therefore, referred to as "underwriters."

It was not long until some of these underwriters realized they were themselves now in a very similar situation to that which they had stepped in to alleviate; that is, many of these individuals were now risking their own personal fortunes on these somewhat risky sea ventures. As a result, some of the individual underwriters began to band together into syndicates.

The syndicates were able to further share the risks (and the profits) and therefore, to accept more of the shipping ventures and/or larger pieces of the individual shipments.

This loosely organized structure of underwriting syndicates became known as the Lloyd's of London Syndicates Structure. Those who were willing to participate in providing financial backing for these enterprises did so by signing their names to a "slip". These individuals were referred to as "Names." Many of the methods established by these early Lloyd's syndicates for offering and accepting risks among themselves are still in use today in the modern Lloyd's enterprises.

Some of the more enterprising Lloyd's underwriters began to recognize that the profits they were making, in assuming some of the risks of these sea-going ventures, might be duplicated if they were willing to assume similar risks for endeavors that did not involve sea voyages.

Certainly, one of the more devastating disasters in the world at this time was the threat of fire destroying homes, businesses, etc. This seemed an obvious opportunity into which the Lloyd's underwriters could expand. Soon, Lloyd's was offering manufacturers, storeowners, and even wealthy homeowners the possibility of offsetting a part of any loss to their property that occurred from fire. Before long these coverages were expanded to encompass some of nature's other perils such as floods and wind damage, and certain man-made perils like robbery and theft.

In the meantime, the shipping industry had found a second harbor – this one in the New World. In New York City, Yankee sea captains and colonial manufacturers began to compete with their British counterparts. Understandably they faced many of the same fears of uninsured risk as did the early English sea entrepreneurs.

As Americans moved westward to seek their fortunes on the expanding frontier, San Francisco became yet another thriving seaport and, accordingly, a second insuring hub in the United States. Thanks to the British attitude that the colonies were no place for English gentlemen to do business, the now thriving Lloyd's enterprises had little desire to export their industry to the new world. The void thus created was not, however, ultimately filled by a structure similar to Lloyd, but rather by independent companies whose entire activity was the agreement to assume part of the risk. The difference here was that the risk takers did not ask for a part of the owners profits, but rather demanded a specific fee for their risk assumption. Thus began the concept of charging an insurance premium, and the insurance industry as we know it today was born.

These two somewhat different competing insurance structures continued to prosper in their own ways, and in their own spheres of concentration, until a major happening occurred in the United

States that would forever change the insurance industry. The happening was the invention of the horseless carriage — the automobile. Perhaps no other single incident has had such a profound and lasting influence on the insurance industry.

Early policies covering automobiles were generally modeled after the policies which had been developed to protect a ship's hull, sails, masts, etc. It was not long before the expanding use and speed of this new mode of transportation suggested the need to also protect people who might be damaged or injured by the use of these automobiles. This gave rise to the concept of Liability Insurance related to automobiles.

Early shipping policies covered the hull; early automobile policies covered the car body. The risk of sinking was insured against by the ship policy; the risk of collision damage was insured under the auto policy. Both recognized the risk of fire. Both recognized the potential for the vessel/vehicle to strike another object and damage that other object. The difference was in how the two policies addressed the amount and type of damage they would cover when such a collision did occur.

At about the same time the new policies were being developed for the horseless carriage, the industrial revolution in America was creating large and, for that period in time, complex industrial companies. As had occurred with the manufacturers and ship owners in London, the American entrepreneurs also realized it would make financial sense to have someone share the risk for many of the pitfalls that might endanger a fast rising business. It wasn't long before the blossoming American insurance industry came forward to offer to protect these business ventures. The Commercial General Liability (CGL) Insurance Policy became the vehicle by which business owners were able to continue to function after encountering certain mishaps.

The CGL policy was designed to protect the owners and stockholders of companies from customers and the public in general. The specifics of the Commercial General Liability Policy will be discussed later in the Specific Coverage Section (Chapter 10). CGL coverage was able to provide emerging manufacturers with a safety net for injuries, or damage to property that their products or employees might cause. Like its predecessor insurance policies, this CGL policy allowed the owners of these companies to apply a specific expense cost factor for their protection, and to diminish the fear that a single incident, or unforeseen series of incidents, could cause the demise of an otherwise thriving business.

In addition to protecting the business owners from claims by the general public during these early days of insurance history, these early CGL policies also protected the owners from claims and lawsuits brought against them by their own employees who were injured on the job. Under such circumstances, the injured worker would be forced to file a claim or lawsuit against his employer, alleging the employer had been negligent and had caused the worker to be injured. This was no different from a member of the general public who could allege the owner of a business had caused an injury.

A substantial difference, however, was that the injured worker often was unable to continue to work after such an injury, and the employer could merely drag out the legal proceedings for such a period of time that the injured worker would have no alternative but to take a meager settlement in order to return to work and support his family. It was not uncommon for business owners to view an injured worker's claim against them as an egregious act of treason. The injured worker was often terminated for such an offensive act, or was fired simply because they were unable to work, even though the cause of the inability was the employment related injury.

Recognizing the inequity of the positions of employer and employee in these work related injury incidents, state legislatures began to enact laws to protect injured workers.

These were almost unanimously referred to as Workmen's Compensation laws, until the concept of political correctness caused the gender offensive term to be changed to Workers' Compensation. These worker related laws provided a number of safeguards to protect an employee injured on the job, while at the same time offering certain relief to the employers bound by these laws. More specific information regarding these WC laws and the employer safeguards can be found in Chapter 5, "Legal Issues." Following the pattern seen in earlier situations, the insurance industry once again quickly stepped in to offer to meet the employer's obligations to an injured worker by creating the Workers' Compensation insurance policy. (See Chapter 12.)

The insurance industry continued to expand along with the American economy. To attempt to simplify the insurance products being called for by their customers, in the mid-1900s the insurers began to combine certain types of policies such as the Personal Fire Policy and the Personal Liability Policy into the Homeowner's Policy (See Chapter 8), and the Commercial Fire Policy and the Commercial General Liability Policy into the Commercial Multi-Peril Package Policy. (See Chapter 11.)

Soon after the emerging insurance industry began to mature, it became apparent that the risks being taken by the insurers could pose the possibility of excessive financial risk. As industrial giants began emerging in the areas of manufacturing, transportation, services, etc., the scope and degree of risk which the insurance companies were assuming could have bankrupt some of them. They needed a mechanism whereby they could transfer a portion of this risk that they had assumed. As a result, insurance companies began to insure their own insurance writings; that is, an insurer would offer to share some of their premium with another insurance company, if that second insurer would agree to also assume some of the potential risk. This concept was called Reinsurance, and is founded on the theory of spreading the risk to maintain financial stability. Reinsurance today is an industry of near equal size, magnitude, sophistication and wealth to the insurance industry itself.

Some companies engaged in these reinsurance enterprises are involved only in the practice of assuming a portion of the risk from the underlying insurer that wrote the business, while agreeing to share in one form or another in certain loss payments. The company that assumes this added risk for a portion of the premium is called the "assumed reinsurer", and the company that agrees to share a portion of its premium with another risk taker is the "cedant" or "ceding company."

Other companies are on both sides of this reinsurance equation; that is, they write the underlying business of protecting their insureds, then become a cedant and seek another company to reinsure their exposure. Under other circumstances, these same companies will become an assumed reinsurer and will accept additional risk from some other underlying or primary insurer.

The result of the insurance companies' drive to provide more and more insurance protection for the people and businesses around the world was that insurers began to offer exotic coverages for almost any type of property or legal activity.

As insurance had grown from many of the other changes and evolutions in lifestyles, the 20th century continued to present needs for other specific protection vehicles. The insurance industry was happy to comply by developing additional new types of sophisticated policies and coverages.

Policies such as the Builders' Risk Policy were introduced to assist those in the business of erecting homes for the growing population, and those who were building the skyscrapers that began to shape the American cities' skylines.

Newly attained levels of personal affluence in America and other parts of the world allowed more and more individuals to become involved with businesses, as investors through the purchase of stocks and bonds. Although initially there was little concern with the quality of management of these large corporate giants now owned by the public, a trend developed that indicated a growing concern with the competence, judgment and results of the directors and officers charged with running these business entities.

Investors — often via class action lawsuits — began to bring claims against these corporations, along with their officers and directors, questioning their competence and performance. The existing insurance carried by the corporations did not extend coverage for such allegations or situations. Directors and Officers Insurance was therefore developed by enterprising insurers and is now one of the staples of the coverages being offered around the world. With this new protection being provided, businesses are able to attain a certain comfort level in the event the corporation, or the individuals functioning as officers and directors, become involved in a policyholder's lawsuit. Most current policies do extend the coverage to the individual directors and/or officers, but not to the corporation upon whose board the directors sit, nor to the specific company employing the officers.

As the general public became more sophisticated, and coincidentally more litigious, claims also began to appear against professionals whose personal relationships had heretofore rendered them almost above being questioned. Physicians, dentists, attorneys, accountants, and architects began to face the fact that everyone for whom they provided their services was not pleased with their efforts. More importantly, some of these disgruntled clients began to do what had been unthinkable previously — they began to sue their personal doctors and lawyers.

This phenomenon in the 1960s and 1970s caused unparalleled growth in the areas of medical malpractice claims and — to a lesser degree — legal malpractice claims. The previously unheard of situation of one physician testifying against another in court (the medical "wall of silence") began to erode, and as more doctors were willing to point accusing fingers at their colleagues, the courts became clogged with patients seeking redress against their physicians and hospitals for actual or perceived errors resulting in less than anticipated medical results. The costs charged by insurers who were willing to provide medical malpractice coverage soared to incredible heights. Many carriers opted to no longer write this type of insurance. Others stayed in the business with premium rates dozen or even hundred of times higher than previous rates.

Certain high-risk medical practitioners found the rates being charged to be prohibitive, and elected to cancel their insurance. This created obvious risk for the doctors caught in such a predicament. It also constituted a difficult situation for the legitimate claimant who was truly entitled to receive compensation for a medical error by a doctor who did not have sufficient assets or insurance to properly compensate the injured party.

Some states enacted legislation to try to mitigate the impact of very high insurance premiums for medical providers, and the extremely large verdicts which were often awarded in cases where juries did find the physician and/or hospital to have violated their duty and responsibility to the patient. In addition to the legislative help provided by some special laws enacted to address this situation, groups of physicians also began to form their own type of insuring organization. By doing so, these professionals could minimize or eliminate the profit margin from the premium rate structure of the insurance companies. They could also be certain these newly formed doctors' insurance companies were run by people who recognized the specific desires of this unified group, and who were conscious of the unique aspects of certain areas related to claims against medical providers.

In more recent times, some large companies and industrial

groups decided they might be able to do without the use of insurers altogether, by combining their individual financial resources to share the risks which had traditionally been assumed by the insurance industry. This concept of being "self insured" is also known as Alternative Risk Transfer.

Under these arrangements, the company or group creates a specific legal Trust, or puts up a bond or other collateral to fund anticipated losses (much the same way an insurance company sets reserves for known and anticipated losses). As with the doctors who formed their own insurance companies, these self-insured companies and groups were able to eliminate the profit aspect from the premium rate structure. The new direction was not, however, without difficulties. One service that insurers provide to their insureds is the handling of the claims and loss investigation. Without the benefit of a conventional insurance policy, self-insured entities needed to assume this function, as well as some others.

A few companies and groups that followed this self-insured path hired their own claims handlers as company employees and became not only self-insured but self-administered, as well. This entailed the creation and maintenance of an entire new department with employee benefits and all other requirements of employee growth.

As an alternative, a collateral industry was born as Third Party Administrators came into being. These private companies would function as independent contractors, and for a fee would handle the claims administration of the self-insured company or group. This eliminated much of the ancillary expense and headaches of self-administration, but again added new costs to the insurance equation — often a primary problem that had led to self-insurance in the first place.

The introduction of self-insurance had an effect on the insurance industry as to the number of policies being written and the premiums being collected. Certain insurance companies were unable to maintain profitability and either ceased doing business, or were taken over by more successful carriers. Nevertheless, the industry continued to thrive, and other new players periodically entered the market.

As with insurance companies, the self-insured entities and groups which were discussed earlier are also often in need of reinsurance protection. The same relationships exist between these self-insured entities and the reinsurers as exists between the reinsurers and the underlying or primary insurance companies that seek their services.

CHAPTER TWO

Types of Insurance Companies

There are several different types of structures under which insurance companies are set up and continue to operate. The most prevalent is the "Stock" insurance company. A stock company is established much like any other corporation. The company is funded by the issuance of shares of stock to investors. The investors may or may not be otherwise associated with the insurance company. That is, any individual investor may be insured by the company in which he has invested, but it is no more a requirement than it is that someone who invests in General Motors drives a GM car. The investors in a stock company make money from dividends as well as stock price increases, and lose money if the price declines.

Again, this is no different than any other business venture in which someone buys stock (ownership) in a company. Investors are generally not interested in the insurance aspects, but rather view their investment as just that — an investment with the motive being to make money.

Investors in stock companies — as with other corporations which issue stock — are allowed to attend stockholders meetings and vote on how the company is run. The majority of insurance companies are stock companies.

Another prevalent type of insurer is a "Mutual" insurance company. In a mutual company, outside investors do not buy shares in the company. Those people who buy an insurance policy from the company own the company. In other words, when a person has an in-force insurance policy with the company, they are also a part owner of the company. If the company is successful during the period of time the policy is in effect, then the company returns a portion of the profits (a "dividend") to those insured during that period.

The people who are the owners of these mutual insurance companies do not invest primarily to make a return on their investment — as with stock company investors. Rather, they are usually interested — and hopeful – that the payment of their original premium will be reduced by way of a rebate, or a partial return of premium, if the company is successful. Their primary interest is generally in buying insurance, and in perhaps receiving a reduction on what they paid as their insurance premium. Outsiders - those not insured with the mutual company — do not own stock, and neither they nor the policy holders can vote on who will run the company or how it will be run.

Many of the carriers who write large numbers of personal insurance policies are set up as mutual companies.

Some companies with large commercial writings are also mutuals, but not nearly as many as are stock companies. In the last few years of the 20th century, a number of mutuals opted to change their structures to that of a stock company. Generally, this allowed the restructured entity to raise additional capital by issuing shares of stock to private investors or the general public, thus obtaining funding from sources other than only their insured group.

Another type of insurer is set up when a group of like-minded, or similarly connected, individuals or companies decide to set up their own insurance company, known as a "Reciprocal" or an "Interinsurance Exchange." Each insured in such an arrangement agrees to insure themselves and all other members of the reciprocal or exchange. For example, a group of physicians may decide to form an insurance company to issue medical malpractice insurance to their own group, and/or to other doctors who may wish to join them. Generally, the group puts up its own money to initially fund the venture.

Reciprocals and interinsurance exchanges may be set up as having "assessable" or "non-assessable" rates. With assessable rates, the members of the reciprocal or exchange may be required to put in additional funding if the initial charges become inadequate to meet their liabilities. If the business is unable to function with the initial capitalization, each member agrees to add additional funds, usually on an annual basis. Conversely, if the company is successful, and makes a profit, the profit is returned to those who were the investors.

If the entity is set up with non-assessable rates, the members have no obligation to make additional investments to salvage the entity if it gets into financial difficulty. In that case, the reciprocal or exchange would have the same recourse to bankruptcy laws, etc., as would any other business venture. With reciprocals or exchanges, there is usually a Trust that is established as the fiduciary controlling the funds that pass through the insurance structure.

Like the mutual company, reciprocals and exchanges are run by and for those being insured. Unlike mutuals, however, which generally market their insurance products to the general public, reciprocals and exchanges usually are limited to groups with similar demographics such as professions, or special interests.

A principal difference, however, between a mutual company and a reciprocal or exchange is that the investors (owners) of the reciprocal or exchange have a risk if the company cannot meet its financial obligations. If you insure with a mutual company, you are an owner of the company and if they are successful you will reap a reward of a reduced or partially rebated premium. If, on the other hand, the mutual company runs out of money, you as an insured have no responsibility to bail them out. With an assessable rated reciprocal or exchange, the participants (insureds) take on the added responsibility of backing the company financially, thus insuring its stability — at least so long as the assets of the individuals last.

Another company structure, very similar to a reciprocal, is called a "Captive" Insurance company. A captive insurer is a company that is formed to insure, generally, one single company or group of companies. Unlike a reciprocal or exchange, which may start up to insure, for example, physicians, and then offers its insurance to other doctors; a captive might be formed by the XYZ Electric Company, a Public Utility, to insure only its own exposures. Or it may be formed by the Acme Grocers Association to insure only those grocers who are already members of the AGA. The captive insurer is usually fully owned by the company or association for which it was formed, and it does not usually offer its products or services to anyone outside of the founding company or association.

A Captive Insurer should be viewed, perhaps, more as an alternative for a company or group being self-insured rather than as an alternative to forming a more conventionally structured insurance company.

In addition to the various types of insurers discussed above, one should also be aware of the existence of companies engaged in the business practice of reinsurance. Many of the companies providing primary and/or excess insurance coverage to the public, may also issue reinsurance to other similar companies. However, there are certain companies that deal primarily, if not exclusively, in providing reinsurance to other insurers, self-insured entities, etc. This reinsurance aspect provides for the primary insurer to diminish some of their exposure to certain risks, spread the danger of large catastrophic losses, or merely to attempt to show they are writing limits higher than is actually the case.

The reinsurance contracts that are placed between the ceding company (the entity that seeks/receives the reinsurance protection) and the assuming company (the carrier that issues the reinsurance contract and assumes the added exposure) can vary widely. There are a number of different kinds of reinsurance that may be placed. These options depend on the needs of the ceding carrier in specific or general situations, and the willingness of the assuming carrier to take on the amount and/or type of exposure that is needed.

A more detailed discussion of the types of reinsurance contracts, and the relationships between cedants and assuming parties, is contained in Chapter 14. Since this entire text is an attempt to provide only basic knowledge of these various subjects, more detailed information relating to the area of reinsurance can be found in other material specifically aimed at this important subject. The company/corporate make-up of an insurer engaged in reinsurance will generally be one of the types mentioned above (stock, mutual, reciprocal or captive.)

Chapter Three

The Players and Their Roles

Insurance is generally sold by three sources: company sales personnel, insurance agents, and insurance brokers. At times, the differentiation among these individuals can be difficult to see or understand.

A company sales person is someone employed by the insurance company to generate "direct" sales to the customer. In most instances, these individuals are truly employees of the company, receiving the same employment benefits as any other company employee. They are generally paid a salary with some sort of sales volume bonus. In almost all situations, the direct sales personnel can only sell insurance for one company — the company by whom they are employed. Direct sales people are most often found at mutual insurers.

In addition to mutual insurers, reciprocals and captives often hire direct employees to market their policies. Since neither of these specialized insurers offers their coverages to the general public, the marketing focus is quite specific and seems to lend itself to having direct employees selling their products.

The vast majority of insurers enlist independent agents to sell their services. These agents are individuals or companies established primarily or exclusively to sell insurance. The people engaged in this endeavor often wear two hats — as agent and as broker.

The insurance agent is usually a company or individual that enters into an agreement with one or more insurance companies to sell the policies of those insurers. The agent is generally at liberty to sell a policy of any of the insurers with whom he has a sales agreement, and they may have dozens of such agreements with all manner of different insurance companies.

Most large stock companies use independent agents to market and sell their policies.

One exception to the independent agent is the company sponsored agency. In this situation, the insurer establishes an insurance agency for the purpose of advancing sales of its own insurance policies. Usually, the agent operating under such an agreement is not truly an "independent" agent, and is committed to attempt to sell the policy of the company that has set up and/or sponsored the agency.

Generally, these special agents are allowed to sell the policies of other companies, but only if the sponsoring insurance company does not offer a specific type of policy needed by the customer, or if the sponsoring company declines to accept the prospective insured. In effect, the sponsoring company has the right of first refusal.

As can be seen, the insurance agent (in its truest sense) is associated with one or more insurance companies. As such, they have certain rights and responsibilities with, and to, the companies they represent.

The insurance broker, on the other hand, generally represents the customer who is seeking insurance. A person or company needing insurance will contact a broker, who will agree to attempt to find an insurance company that will issue the proper type of policy at a price acceptable to the customer. In its purest form, the broker would contact an insurance agent (who represents the insurance companies). They would agree on an insurance company, the proper type policy, and the correct price (the premium). The agent receives a commission from the company for the sale of the policy, and a part of that commission is then passed on to the broker as his payment — a type of "finders fee."

In many instances the agent and broker are one and the same person — or at least two individuals both working for the same agency/brokerage firm. In these situations, the lines of responsibility and authority often become blurred, and at times are not visible at all.

In the purchasing of insurance, it may not seem overly important to specifically determine if the person providing this middleman function is an insurance agent or an insurance broker. The difference can become important if and when problems develop and it is necessary to determine to whom the sales person was primarily responsible — the insurance company or the customer.

Later, in Chapter 5, the legal concepts of Agency and Bailment are explored, and what legal responsibilities these two doctrines impose on someone engaged in an agency relationship with another.

Whether or not the policy is sold by a company sales representative, a company sponsored agency, an independent agent, or a broker, the person with the responsibility to accept or decline a prospective customer is the company underwriter. This is an employee of the insurance company who is familiar with insurable risk, and who is aware of the types of policies the company wishes to write, and the type of insureds they wish to protect. The underwriter has the responsibility to accept or decline a prospective customer as an acceptable risk, and to set the premium needed to insure the risk for the desired coverage.

Since many individuals and companies seek the same basic types of policies and coverages, it is not necessary that the underwriter personally review each and every application for a policy. The insurance companies provide manuals and guidelines, so many of the agents know what types of risk the individual company is willing to insure, what general exceptions might be pertinent, and the price (premium) that will be charged.

In a number of instances, insurance companies provide some of their agents with underwriting authority; that is, the agent can actually accept a risk and bind the company to insure the person or company applying for the policy, without the prior approval of the insurance company. Where the application for insurance does not fit neatly into a predetermined template, the application may need to be submitted to the company underwriter to make the necessary decisions. Except in rare instances, the insureds seldom come into direct contact with the insurance company underwriters.

Another person with whom insureds seldom come into contact is the actuary. The actuary may be an employee of the insurance company or an independent person or firm hired by the insurer for specific functions. The actuary is the person primarily responsible for establishing the premium rates — what everyone will pay for their insurance protection. The rates are established through a series of relatively complex calculations based on the probabilities of a certain type of risk suffering a certain type of loss and sustaining a certain degree of damage. Much of the calculations are based on reviewing past history for identifiable groups of insured types, and extrapolating the past claims history into the future. The anticipated expenses and operating costs are factored into the equations, and it is thereby determined what amount of money will be needed for each type of risk being insured, at various monetary levels of coverage.

Once a policy of insurance is issued, the customer (now the insured) may have little or nothing to do with the insurance company or their representative until the policy expires or is renewed, unless there is a claim to be submitted under the policy. When this occurs, the insured or their representative will deal with the company claims adjuster. The adjuster may be a company employee, or may be the employee of a separate company established to assist the insurance company in handling their claims. These independent adjusters will perform many of the same functions as does a company employee adjuster. The adjuster will gather estimates of the damage, or may personally appraise the damage, to determine how much money will be needed to return the insured, or the damaged third party, back into the same position they were before the loss.

The function of the claims adjuster, either company employee or independent adjuster, will vary somewhat depending upon the type of claim being submitted, the magnitude of the claim, and the geographical location (and legal jurisdiction) where the claim will be handled. Nevertheless, the basic function of the adjuster is to gather the facts surrounding the loss, determine if the situation is one covered by the policy that was purchased by the insured, determine the value of the loss, and settle the matter (if warranted) for a reasonable amount in light of all the above considerations.

The insurance company employee adjusters are paid a salary, as are their other company counterparts. They do not receive compensation based on the amount of the claim or the amount for which the claim is settled. To do so might unduly influence their objectivity and impartiality, with which they are charged in the exercise of their duties. Technically, there is no personal incentive for the adjuster to attempt to reduce the amount of the loss beyond its fair and reasonable size, nor to interpret the coverage provisions of the policy in such a restrictive way as to unreasonably confine the insured's recovery process.

Realistically, one must realize that over zealousness by the adjuster may, however, come into play in trying to please his employer, to the possible detriment of the policyholder. The laws in most states forbid the adjuster from being paid on any contingency basis that might act to offer the adjuster an incentive to view the adjustment process as one of possible personal monetary gain.

Where the insurance company chooses to employ an independent adjuster, rather than use a company employee, this individual also is generally prohibited from working on a contingency basis. As with the company employee, the adjuster should not be tempted to minimize the amount owed to the policyholder or the claimant in order to increase the amount of compensation earned by the adjuster. These independent adjustment companies rely on the insurance companies to hire them to assist in these activities. Again, being realistic, the independent adjuster wishes to please the insurance company with his efforts. This can lead to abuses, and the insurer must be vigilant to see that the involved parties do not receive less than they are owed.

Many states have laws that attempt to further strengthen the requirements that adjusters — whether company employees or independent adjusters — act fairly and impartially when investigating and resolving claims. These laws and requirements are generally referred to a "Fair Claims Practices" and come under the responsibility of the individual state's Department of Insurance.

On the opposite side of the equation from the insurance company employees is the person or company being insured, or their representative. For most of us purchasing personal insurance for our homes, automobiles, lives, etc., we have only ourselves, our friends, or some knowledgeable acquaintance to help us through this seemingly convoluted maze.

Companies seeking to purchase insurance, especially the larger corporations, may have a Risk Manager who is responsible for such decision making. Risk Managers are generally individuals with extensive insurance backgrounds and experience, who are able to compare the various similarities and differences between premium quotes, coverages, etc.

In many cases the claims adjustment experience is an easy and almost effortless process. It is never fun, but it can be relatively painless if everything goes right, and is not complicated by one or more of the large number of possible pitfalls. In some instances, the process breaks down. When this occurs the matter many be moved to a legal or quasi-legal forum; i.e., litigation or arbitration.

The processes of litigation and arbitration are discussed in Chapter 5, "Legal Issues." At this juncture, we need only look at the change in the cast of characters who might become involved when the adjustment process reaches this somewhat strained point.

When an insured or claimant is not satisfied with the position being taken by the insurance company, or disagrees with the amount being offered to resolve the claim, they may seek outside assistance. If the claim is one involving a loss of personal or commercial property, such as a fire, theft, vandalism, etc., the unhappy property owner may engage the service of a Public Adjuster. This should not be confused with an Independent Adjuster, discussed earlier. Although Public Adjusters are also independent, in the sense they are not affiliated with the insurance company, they represent only the insured, while the Independent Adjuster represents the insurance company.

A Public Adjuster is retained almost exclusively in matters of property damage. They seldom, if ever, are used in matters of injury claims. They will re-evaluate the damage, the coverage, and the law that is involved with the particular claim being disputed. The Public Adjuster will generally conduct his own investigation and will do his own appraisal of the amount and scope of the damage being claimed. Unlike the company adjuster and the independent adjuster, the Public Adjuster does usually work on a contingency basis. The higher the Public Adjuster can get the claim amount, generally the more his fee will be. While this can lead to some unscrupulous behavior on the part of some public adjusters, most are only interested in obtaining the full, fair amount that is owed to their clients. In the spirit of today's consumerism, the contingency fee arrangement for a Public Adjuster is seen to be an incentive to attempt to maximize the return to the insured/claimant.

The involvement of a Public Adjuster may not be sufficient to resolve a disputed claim. If the Public Adjuster cannot convince the insurance company to settle the matter, there are still some other options available. Most insurance policies contain Appraisal and Arbitration Clauses. These mandate that the insured will submit any first party, irresolvable claim to an appraisal process, and ultimately, if necessary, to arbitration. In some instances, when arbitration cannot resolve the issues, the dispute may become a matter to be heard by the courts.

The flow of activity related to the claim that goes into arbitration or litigation will also be discussed in more detail in Chapter 5, "Legal Issues."

Some insurance companies and some self-insured organizations hire a third party administrator (TPA) to handle their claims for them. These independent firms are usually under contract to the insurance company or self-insured group to perform many of the same functions as would the insurance company claims adjuster.

The TPA adjuster functions basically the same as the company adjuster described above, but is the employee of an independent firm representing the interests of the self-insured entity or the insurance company.

Another insurance company employee with whom the insured may come into contact is the Loss Control Specialist. The dealings between the insured and the Loss Control Specialist are generally much less adversarial than is the interaction with the claims adjuster.

The Loss Control Specialist is someone with knowledge of the insurance aspects, but who also is experienced in areas such as engineering. A more appropriate term for these individuals might be loss prevention specialist. Their job is to work with the insured to attempt to minimize the frequency and severity of accidents suffered by the insured. Obviously, this usually only involves those larger companies that have a number of claims and/or the potential for large or catastrophic losses.

Since the premium large corporations are charged for their insurance is very often related to their loss history, the task of reducing the size of the losses or the number of claims may have a corresponding reduction in what the insured pays for its insurance. Obviously, most companies are eager to receive such help from these insurance company representatives. Entire loss prevention programs are installed in some companies that can have a dramatic impact on the losses suffered by the company, and/or their employees.

In the discussion above, relating to disputes between insureds and the insurers, involving claims adjusters, public adjusters, and arbitrators, the issues involved settlement of claims related to the insured's own property or damages (a first party loss). On occasion, the dispute does not involve a disagreement between the insured and his insurance company, but rather it involves a third party — someone alleging damages caused by the insured, and for which the insured is protected under a liability insurance contract. Such a claim is a third party claim and involves someone alleging to have been damaged or injured by the insured, and seeking a monetary settlement as compensation for those damages or injuries.

An injured third party, alleging negligence on the part of the insured that caused the damages, will submit a claim to the insured or directly to the insured's insurer. The insurance company will, in effect, "stand in the shoes of the policyholder." The insurance company will analyze the coverage provided under the applicable insurance policy, and if coverage exists, will initiate the adjustment process.

Generally, a third party claimant submits his damages to the company or independent adjuster assigned by the company to handle the loss. The adjuster investigates the circumstances of the accident, determines if the facts fit within the confines of the coverage afforded by the insured's policy, and then verifies the validity of the submitted damages. In the vast majority of situations, the adjuster is able to resolve the claim directly with the claimant for an amount of money with which both parties are satisfied.

Unfortunately, there are occasions when an amicable settlement is not possible, the third party claimant retains a lawyer, and may ultimately file a lawsuit or other legal proceeding against the insured.

Depending on the type of insurance policy written by the company for the insured, there is generally coverage for legal fees in almost all primary liability type insurance policies. (Note there are also excess liability type policies, many of which do not provide for legal expenses in all cases. These excess coverages are discussed further, in Chapter 13.)

The primary insurer generally has an obligation to provide (and pay for) a defense of the insured if the allegations of the lawsuit fall within the parameters of the policy coverage language. Under such circumstances, the insurance company refers the lawsuit to an attorney to file the necessary appearance on behalf of the insured, and to defend the matter. The attorney may be an employee of the insurance company (referred to as "house counsel") or may be an independent attorney or law firm which the insurance company engages to defend their insured for this specific law suit.

Although the lawyer is generally hired and paid for his services by the insurance company, the attorney's responsibility is to the insured, not to the insurance company. On occasion, a conflict will arise between the insured and the insurer. Under those circumstances, the attorney hired to defend the insured has a clear and specific duty to represent only the position of the insured, even if that position may be contrary to the best interest of the insurance company that is paying him.

Nevertheless, there are certain instances in which the insured may be entitled to separate counsel — selected by the insured, but paid for by the carrier — to specifically represent the interests of the insured in matters that may or may not be covered under the policy. (See the Glossary at the end of this book for " Cumis Counsel.")

CHAPTER FOUR

The Basic Policy Format

Almost all standard insurance policies are constructed the same way. They have five general parts: The Declarations, the Insuring Agreement, the Exclusions, the Conditions, and the Endorsements. Various insurers may use somewhat different presentations of one or more of these policy parts, but the content and purpose of each is very consistent from insurance company to insurance company.

The Declarations Page is what makes a particular insurance policy for one insured different from all other policies issued by the insurer. It is here that the insured's name is indicated, along with the address and other identifying information.

The Declarations Page contains the policy number. Universally, each policy issued by a particular insurance company bears an identifying policy number. The policy numbers bear no similarity from one company to another. Some may use only numbers; other will use a combination of numbers and letters; some may use a specific letter or number prefixes to identify the type of policy being issued; some may use a suffix number to indicate such things as the number of renewals this policy has gone through. Although every company has its own method of sequencing the policy numbers, all companies use some numbering system to identify the specific policy issued.

Also on the Declarations Page, the general coverages being insured are listed. Again, companies may vary on how they display this information; however, the coverages being purchased by the insured are shown here in one form or another.

If a policy contains a deductible provision, for one or more of the coverages being provided, the deductible information should be shown on the Declarations Page.

Similarly, the identity of any Loss Payees (See Glossary) under the policy, and/or Additional Named Insureds (See Glossary) under the policy, may also be shown on the declarations page. The term of the policy, or length of time the policy will be in effect, from Inception Date to Expiration Date is shown here.

Also on the Declarations Page, the specifics of the property being insured are identified, by address, physical description, etc.

Although the specific endorsements to a policy are contained in, or affixed to, the policy, and spell out the parameters of the endorsement language, the existence of the endorsements related to a particular policy are generally identified on the Declaration Page by listing the endorsements names and/or numbers.

Finally, the Declarations Page shows the premium being charged for the coverage being provided. The premium may appear as a single inclusive number, or may be broken down to show the charges related to specific coverages contained in the policy.

Since the Declarations Page is often the only thing that changes from one policy period to the next, at renewal many carriers merely issue a new Declarations Page, rather than reissuing the entire policy contract.

The main body of the insurance policy is the <u>Insuring Agreement</u>. It is here that the perils being insured against are set forth and defined. The type of policy being issued determines whether the perils include those that are usually associated with damage to ones own property, or to property of others, or to acts the insured might commit which could damage other people or property. (Refer to Part II, "Specific Coverages" for a better understanding of specifically what coverages are provided under different types of insurance policies.)

In policies covering the insured's own property, the type of property is often elaborated upon. Although certain property may be specifically identified in the Declarations Page, the description contained in the Insuring Agreement is usually only general in nature. It may indicate the location of certain real property, the geographical boundaries of certain operations being covered, the description of a particular piece of property, or the activities for which the insured is being insured.

The Insuring Agreement will generally explain what the duties, rights and responsibilities of the parties will be in the event of a claim under the policy. It may cover the time frame in which a claim must be presented, whether the insured will be required to present a "proof of loss" form, whether the insured may sue the company in court if disputes arise or if they must seek redress through the arbitration process.

In liability policies, the Insuring Agreement generally states that the company has the duty and the obligation to defend the insured from all claims filed against them, even if those claims are without merit, and to indemnify or pay for any judgment rendered against the insured in such claim or lawsuit. The company usually has the right (but not the obligation) to investigate any claim submitted by the insured or by a third party.

There is generally a Cooperation Clause within the Insuring Agreement that requires the insured to assist the insurer in all reasonable ways toward resolution of any loss sustained and covered by the policy.

After providing in the Insuring Agreement what the insurance policy covers, the policy then limits some of those broad promises in the Exclusions section of the policy. While the Insuring Agreement is usually general in nature, the Exclusions are usually quite specific.

It is necessary to limit the coverage being provided for a number of reasons. Most specifically, if coverage is normally provided in other types of policies, the Exclusions will attempt to eliminate that article, activity, or result from the coverage. The intent is to avoid double recovery wherever possible.

Exclusions in a first party or property policy might indicate that the property being insured will not be covered for such things as wear & tear, inherent vice, latent defects, etc. Coverage for real property might have limitations for damage arising out of settling, shifting, bulging of foundations, walls, etc. Very often damage resulting from earth movement (such as earthquakes) is not covered unless it is specifically addressed elsewhere in the policy. Flood damage, or damage from other surface water, may be excluded. Although theft may be a covered peril, any "mysterious disappearance" of an article may not be recoverable under the policy unless it is specifically described and mentioned as being covered. (That is to say the coverage would not be in effect unless it can be shown the article was specifically taken from a known place at a known time.) Since there may be a substantial increase in the risk of damage to property that is unoccupied for long periods of time, many policies covering buildings contain an exclusion for damage to alienated premises.

In General Liability policies, there is usually an exclusion for injury to a third party arising out of the loading or unloading of a motor vehicle. Injuries of this type are usually covered by the automobile policy, and the General Liability policy exclusion attempts to avoid duplicating that coverage.

General Liability policies often exclude damage arising out of professional services rendered by the insured, since such coverage is better provided by professional liability insurance contracts such as an Errors & Omissions policy, or some specific professional malpractice policy. Similarly, since providers of alcoholic beverages can purchase Liquor Legal Liability coverage, the General Liability policy usually excludes liability arising out of such activities.

Since the insured may purchase first party coverage to provide for perils to property that the insured may own, or be holding for some reason, the General Liability and Automobile Liability policies generally exclude damage to property in the care, custody, or control of the insured.

Workers' Compensation coverage is available to almost all employers, so the Automobile and General Liability policies exclude injuries to employees of the insured if they are injured during the course and scope of their employment. This is an important exclusion because many Automobile Liability policies, and premises liability policies, contain Medical Payments coverage. This pays certain medical costs incurred by anyone injured while in the insured automobile, or on the insured premises, regardless of whether or not the injury was caused by the negligence of the insured. Without a Workers' Compensation exclusion, an injured worker, under certain circumstances, might be able to collect under Workers' Compensation and also under the automobile or premises policy of his employer.

The final section making up the basic insurance policy is the

Conditions. Here the insurance company sets forth the contract terms. There may be certain limitations to the coverage being provided – not to be confused with specific exclusions. There is usually a "liberalization" clause, which, in effect, says if the insurance company issues the same type of policy that broadens or expands the coverage, the existing (previously issued) policy will be broadened to provide the revised degree and type of coverage.

This allows the company to conform, for instance, to court directed interpretations of certain policy terms and conditions, without the need to recall and reissue all existing policies that might be affected by the court's ruling. The clause can also be used by the company on a voluntary basis for marketing purposes to enhance the coverage being provided to its current policyholders.

The Conditions Section will specify how, and for what reasons, either party may cancel the policy. Generally, the insured may cancel the policy at any time and for any reason. The only question that arises in such circumstances is how much, if any, of the unearned but paid premium will be returned to the policyholder. The insurance company, on the other hand, does not have the luxury of such a broad escape route from an unprofitable or high risk contract.

Once the policy is issued, the insurer normally can only cancel the contract for failure of the insured to pay the premium (see "Consideration" under the Contract Section of Chapter 5 on "Legal Issues"), or if the insurer can show that fraud was committed by the insured in the purchase of the policy. Such restrictions are often similar for the insurers' rights to not renew a policy that is expiring, although some policies and state insurance laws only deal with "mid-term" cancellations. A number of states, through their insurance laws and regulations, have imposed restrictions regarding the insurer's rights to cancel and/or non-renew policies.

Since laws and customs may vary dramatically in other countries, insurance companies in the United States may often limit, in the

Conditions Section, the geographical territory where the policy will be in effect. This may not be pertinent to stationary, real property; however, many things are mobile and may be physically situated in an area where the risk is substantially higher than was contemplated by the insurer when the policy was written.

The same is true for liability policies that cover the insured's actions. While certain activities may be relatively risk free in some parts of the world, other countries may impose harsh legal or civil penalties for those same actions. The territory conditions attempt to limit the insurance company's liability to the risks in known territories that they considered when the policy was issued.

As with most contracts, the parties entering into the agreement do not want the rights or obligations given over to some other party without full mutual agreement to do so. This is called a Contract Assignment, and the conditions section of the policy restricts the insured from assigning their rights and obligations unless the insurer agrees. An insurance policy is an agreement for the insurer to protect (monetarily) the property and/or actions of the insured, and is based on what the insurer knows and is told about the insured. If the insured's character or makeup changes materially after the policy is issued; i.e., the insured entity is sold to another owner, the risk to the insurer could be substantially altered. In those situations the Assignment Clause would allow the insurer, in effect, to renegotiate the terms and price of the policy to better reflect the changed risk factors.

In many types of policies, the insurer pays for loss to the insured's property, even though the damage may have been caused by the negligent actions of some other party. The person whose property was damaged (in this case the insured), would have the right to seek compensation for the damage from the negligent party. However, they may opt to collect from their own insurance company, and give the insurer the right to proceed against the wrongdoer to collect some or all of what the insurer paid to its insured. This is called Subrogation, and the rights of the insurance company to step into the shoes of its policyholder to recoup their loss is found in the Conditions Section of the policy. (Subrogation is discussed further in Chapter 5, "Legal Issues".)

For commercial policies, the insurance company obtains the right, in the Conditions Section, to inspect and audit certain aspects of the companies they agree to insure. This is in the Inspection and Audit clause of the Condition Section. As mentioned above, it is possible that the entity originally insured may have materially changed since the inception of the policy. Those changes could alter the risk that the insurance company thought they were taking. The right to periodically take another look at what was insured is given to the insurer in this clause.

One of the very important, and most frequently used, clauses in the Conditions Section of liability policies is the Other Insurance Clause. As was discussed earlier in this chapter, insurance companies attempt to avoid (in most circumstances) the duplication of payment to an injured or damaged party, whether that party is the insured or a third party. In addition to some of the specific exclusions in the policy that seek to eliminate such overlapping payments, the Other Insurance Clause is designed to deal with two or more policies which provide substantially the same coverage to the same person or entity for the same incident. Such situations can arise not only because an entity may have bought duplicating policies, but also from having coverage extended under someone else's policy (as when the named insured under one policy is also entitled to coverage as an additional insured under someone else's policy.)

When such potentially duplicative coverage arises, the Other Insurance Clause attempts to set forth how the co-existing policies will each respond to the claim. Generally speaking, there are three types of other insurance clauses: Pro-Rata, Equal Shares, and Exculpatory.

In a Pro-Rata clause, the policy says that if more than one policy provides coverage for a specific claim or loss, the policies will share the loss on the basis that their individual limits of liability bear to the total of all applicable limits of liability. For instance, if there are two policies which will share the loss, and one has a limit of liability of $100,000 while the other has a $200,000 limit, the first carrier will pay one third of the loss and the other will pay two thirds.

The Equal Shares clause says that if there are two or more policies providing coverage for the same loss, the policies will each respond equally, up to the limits of their respective limits of liability. In the example above with two policies, one at $100,000 and the other at $200,000 limits of liability, each would pay an equal amount up to a maximum of $ 100,000 each (the limits of the lower policy), and then the remaining carrier(s) would respond to the additional payments necessary to settle the loss.

An Exculpatory Clause says that if there is other viable insurance that will address the loss, the coverage under this policy shall be excess to all other collectible insurance. In other words, if the insured has other coverage available to them, whether in a policy they purchased or one purchased by someone else in which they qualify as an insured, the policy with the exculpatory language would not respond at all until all other insurance was exhausted.

Any of these three clauses works well, so long as all policies that are being called upon to respond to a loss contain compatible types of Other Insurance Clauses. Certainly if all the policies contain Pro Rate clauses, or Equal Shares clauses, the sorting out of the respective responsibilities is relatively simple. Things get a little less clear when the responding policies have conflicting wording, or where all policies have exculpatory clauses.

The laws governing the interpretation of these conflicting clauses vary somewhat from state jurisdiction to jurisdiction. There are, however, some generally accepted rules for solving these apparent conflicts. If one or more of the policies has a pro-rata clause, but one or more has an equal shares clause, the coverage will generally be allocated by equal shares. When one policy has a pro-rata or an equal shares clause, with the other policy having an exculpatory clause, the pro-rata policy will be primary and the exculpatory policy will be excess. If both (all) policies have exculpatory clauses, the insured cannot be left without primary coverage, and the usual interpretation is for the policies with exculpatory language to share the loss on a pro-rata basis.

Since there is much in an insurance policy to be interpreted, the Conditions often include definitions on certain terms found in the policy.

A general rule to remember when reviewing an insurance policy is that it is a legal contract. As with any contract, it is important to read the entire form, rather than reading only one particular clause or paragraph that may appear to cover the aspect in which you are interested. As has been seen from the foregoing information, the construction of the policy may very well provide coverage in one place, and then remove it in another.

CHAPTER FIVE

Legal Issues

(AUTHOR'S NOTE: As mentioned in the Preface of this manual, the material contained herein, and especially in the following chapter, is not intended to provide legal advice, nor should it be construed as practicing law. These areas are the purview of the attorneys within the legal community. For specific legal advice or to discuss a particular legal matter, a licensed attorney should be contacted.)

CONTRACTS

All legal and binding contracts are comprised of three basis ingredients: an offer by one party to do or refrain from doing something (the OFFER); an agreement or acceptance by another party of the offer (the ACCEPTANCE); and the conveying of something of value (the CONSIDERATION) from one party to the other in order to bind the contract, and make it a legal and enforceable document. There must also be "a meeting of the minds"; i.e., a mutual understanding of what is involved.

An insurance policy is a contract entered into between a person wishing to be protected from certain monetary losses (the INSURED), and an insurance company (the INSURER) that agrees, for a price (the PREMIUM), to accept part or all of the insured's risk.

In the case of an insurance policy, an insurer offers to accept certain potential risks which are foreseeable, and for which the insured wishes to be insulated. These offers take the form of advertisements, solicitations by the companies themselves, and/or solicitations by agent, brokers, or sales representatives. Generally speaking, these offers by the insurance industry and their representatives cover basic risks, which most people face in their day to day personal and business lives. Offers to write other more esoteric types of insurance are also solicited by insurance companies, agents and brokers, and are often found in trade magazines or other industry periodicals.

An individual or company wishing to take advantage of these insurance company offers will usually contact the company or the agent, and be provided an application form of some sort. The form will request details about the individual or entity that is to be insured, the type of insurance being requested, and certain historical data regarding past insurance and claims activity. This information is necessary for the underwriters and actuaries to determine if this person or company fits into the insurer's anticipated universe of prospective insureds, and to determine the appropriate premium to be charged for the coverage being written.

If the insurer feels comfortable with the information obtained from the insurance buyer, and if the prospective insured likes what the company is offering, as well as the premium being charged, the two parties will enter into a contract. The contract is the policy itself, and the consideration to bind the contract is the premium.

As indicated above, there must also be a meeting of the minds of the parties as to what each party is to do or not do, and each party will have specific duties, rights and obligations under the terms of the contract. It is expected that each party will honor their respective obligations and will perform their duties under the covenant of good faith and fair dealing that all contracts require.

AGENCY AND BAILMENT

Two legal concepts with which the insurance industry deals on a regular basis are "agency" and "bailment." The legal term "agency" should not be confused with the term describing a person or company that sells insurance (an insurance agency). The individual who earns his or her living working at an insurance agency selling insurance, may or may not be a legal agent of an insurance company or some other entity. The term "agent" has somewhat different meanings in these two contexts. (See Chapter 3, "The Players and Their Roles")

It is easier to understand the concept of legal agency, and the process by which someone acts as an agent for another, if the word "agent" is replaced by the word "servant." The concept of legal agency reverts back to older times when many people did engage servants to do their bidding. These employees were often the personal representatives of their "masters", and the earliest mention of the agency theory of liability was termed the "master-servant doctrine."

In effect, the theory of agency says that if a person is functioning at the direction of, and for the primary purpose of, another, the first person is the agent of the other, who is referred to as the principal. In such situations, the principal is held accountable, under the law, for the actions of the agent. The principal may not shield himself from responsibility by asserting the actions were done by another, if that other person was the principal's agent.

The agency relationship exists most frequently in matters of employment. When a company hires an employee, that employee is in an agency relationship with the employer so long as his actions are confined to the functions for which he was hired. The employee, as the agent of the employer, may do something, or refrain from doing something, which will impose a legal liability on the employer, even though the employer may have been totally unaware of the specific action or lack of action taken by the employee.

The theory that the principal (or master) will be held accountable for the actions of the agent (or servant) is called *respondeat superior*. In many jurisdictions, when the principal is held to be responsible in these agency relationships, the courts have allowed the principal to seek redress from the agent if the actions were not the type that the principal should have reasonably foreseen, or if the agent's actions were beyond the scope of the agreement between the agent and the principal.

At times, the court will hold a principal accountable for the acts of his agent even if those actions are well beyond the principal's directions, or even if the agent's actions were contradictory to the instructions of the principal. This is allowed to happen if the agent has the <u>appearance</u> of functioning as the agent of the principal, and a third party relies on that appearance. This is called "ostensible authority", and means that the general public may have the right to assume an agency relationship exists if a person reasonably appears to be functioning as the agent of someone else, and if there seems to be evidence of this agent/principle relationship.

A second legal relationship, which, at times, exists between people, is a bailment. Unlike an agency relationship, a bailment is created when the relationship comes into existence not for the primary purpose of helping one of the parties (as with an agency relationship), but for a mutual benefit of both parties. This distinction is not always clear. Often a bailment arises when one party entrusts another with property for a specific purpose, such as a dry cleaner accepting someone's clothing, or an automobile mechanic being given a persons car to service. In these types of situations, although the owner of the property is deriving some value from the temporary conveyance of the property, it is actually for the mutual benefit of both parties. Certainly, an employee is benefiting from his employment; however, the primary benefit falls to the employer who is reaping the harvest of the employee's labor.

Unlike an agent-principal relationship, a person in a bailment relationship with another cannot be held accountable for the acts of the other party. While a dry cleaner may possess the clothes of someone in order to clean them and return them to the owner — and is therefore in a bailment with the clothing owner — a person who is given clothing to sell by a clothing manufacturer would probably be functioning in an agency relationship with the manufacturer.

One of the classic scenarios in which insurance companies need to determine agency vs. bailment involves someone driving the automobile of another. In almost all automobile insurance policies (as will be seen in the Part II, Chapter 7, "Specific Coverages"), so long as the driver of a vehicle is operating the vehicle with the permission of the owner, the policy will cover the actions of that driver. Nevertheless, there are situations that arise when it is critical to determine if a person, even though driving with the owner's permission, was an agent of the owner.

If an accident occurs under these circumstances, so long as the damages are within the limits of liability of the insurance policy, the insurer will respond (all other facts being non-contested in our example.) The claim should be disposed of regardless if the injured or damaged party brings the claim against the owner, driver, or both.

The question of agency does come into play, however, if the policy limits are insufficient to satisfy the total damages caused by the permissive user of the vehicle. In that situation, the owner may well have an exposure beyond the limits of his insurance policy if the driver was in an agency relationship with him at the time of the accident. On the other hand, if the driver was operating the vehicle with the owner's permission, but not on any errand or purpose for the owner's benefit (thus failing to meet the standard for establishing agency), then the owner should not be responsible for any of the damages whatsoever. The owner's insurance policy would still respond to the claim against the permissive user of the vehicle, and to the claim against the owner. However, under the law, in the absence of agency existing, the absentee owner of the vehicle should not be held accountable.

Another common situation where the question of agency and bailment comes into play with insurance claims involves the question of subrogation. Under the provisions of most insurance policies (See Part II, "Specific Coverages"), if an insurer is called upon to pay for certain damages to property of their insured, the insurer obtains the rights to proceed against any other party who may have caused the damage. In other words, had the property owner not possessed insurance on the property, or opted to not collect for their damage under the policy, the property owner would have the right to proceed against whoever damaged their property. By choosing to have the insurance company repair or pay for the damaged property, the property owner agrees to allow the insurer to proceed against the other party in order to recoup their loss payment. The insurance company is said to be subrogated to the rights of their insured.

In subrogation claims, as with all others, the issues of contributory negligence or comparative negligence, discussed later in this chapter, come into play. These issues deal with the question of who was at fault and to what degree. If the owner of the damaged property was totally or partially at fault in causing the damage to their own property, the ability of the insurance company to recover their payment from some other party may be severely limited.

Therefore, if the property was in the possession of someone

other than the owner, it is critical to know the relationship between the owner and the person possessing the property at the time of the damage.

Under an agency relationship, the negligence of the agent is imputed to the principal. Therefore, if the property was in the possession of someone who was functioning as the agent of the owner, that agent's negligence can be used against the owner (and the subrogating insurance company) in defeating or mitigating the claim against the negligent party. On the other hand, if the person possessing the property at the time it was damaged was in a bailment situation with the owner, any negligence on the part of the bailee cannot be imputed to the owner, so the bailee's negligence should have no bearing on the claim by the owner (or their insurance company) against the other party who caused or contributed to the damage.

A person who is given property to care for, or on which to perform a specific function, is usually in a bailment situation with the owner of the property. As such, the accepting party is expected to exercise reasonable care and diligence in protecting the property from damage. A dry cleaner accepting a customer's clothes is in a bailment situation. A veterinarian accepting a pet to groom would be in a bailment. The driver of the car in our above example would be expected to take reasonable precautions to protect the car from damage while in a bailment situation.

While in an agency relationship it might be hoped the agent would exercise a high degree of care. The law generally does not recognize the liability for any failure to care for the property, because if the agent were negligent in caring for the property, the principal would be equally responsible for that negligence. It would be as if the principal would have damaged the property himself. (Recourse does exist in some jurisdictions between agent and principal. Under the interpretation of the doctrine of *respondeat superior*, some courts have ruled a principal has the right to expect the agent to exercise the same degree of care over the principal's property as he would otherwise show to his own.)

It is possible for two individuals to be involved in an agency relationship, which will evolve into a bailment, then back to agency, and so on. Using the automobile scenario again, a permissive user of an automobile may be given a car to use by the owner to run a specific errand for the owner. While the driver is going from point A to point B to accomplish the owner's errand, he would most probably be in an agency relationship with the owner. Let us then suppose the driver decides to not return directly back to the owner's location, but instead (with the owner's permission) detours to pick up his own laundry. During this side trip the driver would still be covered by the owner's automobile policy because he was operating the vehicle with the owner's permission; but since the side trip has no apparent benefit to the owner, the driver would be operating the vehicle under a bailment. The owner should not be held personally accountable if the driver causes an accident during this personal detour.

Continuing the scenario, if the driver runs a second errand on behalf of the owner, after picking up his laundry, and is in the process of returning the vehicle to the owner following this second errand for the owner, the driver most probably would be back into an agency relationship, with the owner being held accountable for the driver's actions. It should be noted that legal jurisdictions differ as to whether or not the driver would enter into the agency relationship as soon as he completed his personal errand and began to proceed to the owner's second errand, or if the agency relationship would not reattach to the relationship until after the driver had actually begun the second errand, rather than just traveling to it.

TORT LIABILITY

In almost all jurisdictions in the United States, the courts apply what is referred to as English Common Law. (One notable exception is the State of Louisiana, where Napoleonic Law is the rule of the land.) English Common Law is a body of laws that originally emanated from England, and were exported to America as the settlers began to arrive in the New World. The laws evolved from judges hearing cases in the English countryside, deciding right from wrong, and assessing damages where called for. As more and more cases were heard, case similarities emerged. The judges, attempting to rule consistently on similar cases with similar issues, wrote down their finding for their own future usage as well as for other judges confronted with similar issues. The rulings were amended as new issues and questions arose over the years.

Common law is different from Statutory Law. In addition to the local judges making rulings on fact situations, occasionally legislative bodies (Parliament and local boroughs in England; Congress, state legislatures, city counsels, etc., in the U.S.) will pass laws to govern certain circumstances. These statutes provide for the rendering of decisions based on specific sets of circumstances.

Courts use both common law and legislative statutory law to decide liability and damages in civil litigation. When a person or legal entity believes they have been injured or damaged by the actions of another, they may make a claim against the allegedly offending party to recoup their damages. Liability is assessed by first determining if the offending party was negligent in his actions. Negligence is generally defined as having a duty to do something, or refrain from doing something, and then violating that duty.

The mere existence of negligence does not, in most situations, however, automatically impose liability. The two terms are not synonymous. A person's or entity's negligence must be the Proximate Cause of the damage or injury to another. That is not to say the negligence must be the only cause, or the primary cause, but it must be the proximate cause. The proximate cause is a continuous sequence of events, unbroken by any intervening cause, that results in injury or damages that would not have otherwise occurred. Even though a person has violated a duty, unless that duty violation was the proximate cause of the injury or damage, the negligent party is not liable for the injury or damage.

As an example, it is against the law to operate a motor vehicle while under the influence of drugs or alcohol. As automobile drivers, everyone has a duty to not operate a motor vehicle while impaired by alcohol or drugs. If a driver were operating a vehicle while legally intoxicated (thus violating a duty owed), he would be negligent. However, if another driver struck the inebriated driver's vehicle which was proceeding legally, the inebriated driver's negligence would not have been the proximate cause of the accident, even though the driver who was "under the influence" would have been negligent. Without the proximate cause bridge, the issue of liability would not be complete and the injured party could not collect for damages against the inebriated driver.

In order to determine the existence of legal liability, there is still yet another step (beyond negligence and proximate cause) that must be established. This is the issue of Contributory Negligence or Comparative Negligence. These are two similar, yet differing, legal concepts.

The doctrine of contributory negligence says, in effect, that if the damaged or injured party was negligent along with the party against whom a claim or lawsuit has been brought, the injured or damaged party cannot collect for any damages sustained. In jurisdictions recognizing this legal concept, contributory negligence is said to be "a bar to recovery"; i.e., any negligence whatsoever on the part of the claimant would keep that claimant from receiving any recovery.

Although this may seem somewhat harsh, it is one of the principles that were brought to the United States from the English Common Law system. Anyone contributing to his or her own difficulty had to bear their own entire loss.

In the mid-to-late 20th century, several state legislatures began to think of this old established doctrine as being harsh. As a result, states began to enact legislation that would temper the damage assessment. The new laws were called "Comparative Negligence" laws. They attempted to limit the damages that an injured party could receive if that injured party had also contributed to the accident that caused their own damages, without barring all recovery.

The basic premise of these new laws was to reduce the amount of the damages an injured party could receive by the same proportion that their own negligence contributed to the accident. The comparative negligence laws fall primarily into two distinct types.

One set of these laws asks the jury, or other trier of the facts, to determine the amount each party contributed to the 100% of the negligence that brought about the accident. The proportion of the damages that could be recovered is the same as the proportion of the adverse party's negligence. In other words, if the plaintiff (or claimant) was found to be 25% negligent, and the defendant was 75% negligent, then the claimant would only receive 75% of the full value of their claim. This meant that if a claimant were even 99% at fault for their own damages, they could still recover 1% from the other party. This is called Pure Comparative Negligence.

Another type of comparative negligence laws that was enacted in some states attempted to maintain the scales a little more equitably. These laws followed the same type of logic for assessing damages when both parties were at fault; however, any party who was more than 50% at fault could not collect for any of their damages from the other party. This is referred to as Modified Comparative Negligence.

As was mentioned earlier, laws and statutes enacted by legislatures also sought to amend certain other aspects of the Common Law. By legislative decree in some states, certain minors or people with diminished mental capacity are not held accountable for their actions in common law. This generally also applies to the enforceability of contracts that are entered into by minors or incompetent individuals. There is no real unanimity as to what age a person reaches their legal age of majority and is no longer considered a minor in matters of civil law. Some states have set the age at 21, others at 18, and others still younger. Some states have determined that small children (under the age of 7 years old, for instance) cannot be held accountable for their actions, while other youngsters over the age of 14 will be held accountable. For actions involving children between 7 and 14 in these jurisdictions, the judge or jury must determine whether the child was fully aware of their actions, and the resultant consequences that followed.

Many states also have specific legislation dealing with products that cause damage. A product that is found to be inherently dangerous would fall under the doctrine of Strict Liability. Under such a doctrine, the manufacturers, distributors and retailers who place such products into the stream of commerce are held strictly liable and lose many of the same defenses as would be available to other entities or manufactures. Generally, contributory negligence and often comparative negligence theories are not allowed in cases where manufacturers or others are held to be strictly liable.

A similar defense available in many civil law suits is Assumption of Risk, which states that a person is not responsible for injury or damage to another if the damaged person puts himself or herself at risk and is thereby injured. This defense is also not generally allowed in matters of strict liability. In some jurisdictions, a products liability claim involving strict liability would switch the burden of proof from the plaintiff (who would normally have the burden of proving the defendant's negligence), to the defendant who would be required to prove the product had not been negligently manufactured, and was not inherently dangerous.

LEGAL ACTIONS

Civil Litigation:

When an accident occurs, the injured party usually begins their dealings with a representative of the insurance company. (See Chapter 3, "The Players and Their Roles"). The vast majority of claims that occur, and for which insurance coverage exists, are settled between the damaged individual and the insurance company. Although the number of claims that are not amicably settled (without resorting to any type of legal action) varies from jurisdiction to jurisdiction, experience shows this number to be relatively small. Nevertheless, there are times when the parties cannot agree — either on issues of liability or damages — and the claimant must either withdraw, or resort to other available avenues.

One of the choices available for further remedy is to file a lawsuit in the appropriate venue; i.e., the court area that has jurisdiction over the matter. A lawsuit may be filed by an attorney licensed to represent others, or may be filed on one's own behalf. This is said to be "in pro per" (in *propria persona*), or "in one's own person."

The filing of a legal action must be done timely. In all court jurisdictions, there are legislative statutes governing the time, following an incident that gives rise to the lawsuit, in which the legal proceedings must begin. Various types of incidents — property damage, bodily or personal injury, contract disputes, medical or legal malpractice, financial transactions, etc. - - each has a specified time period in which the action must be filed. These time periods - - called the Statute of Limitations — differ from jurisdiction to jurisdiction, and for the different types of incidents. (There are similar Statutes of Limitations governing criminal charges as well as civil actions; however, we are not dealing with these criminal matters within this text.)

The commencement of a lawsuit usually involves filling out a summons and/or complaint, or bill of particulars. It is in this document that the plaintiff makes the allegations of wrongdoing and negligence by the defendant(s). The complaint usually contains a section wherein the plaintiff indicates the means and amount of redress being sought in the lawsuit; i.e., money damages, injunctive relief, etc.

After the complaint is filled out, it must be filed with the clerk of the court, and usually a small fee is charged. The filing of the complaint itself is insufficient to activate the process. It is necessary to see that the party being sued is presented with (served) a copy of the complaint, along with a summons to appear in court to answer the charges.

Having once been served with the summons and complaint, the defendant must file an answer to the charges within a specified period of time, or request an extension of that time to answer. This may also be done by the defendant hiring an attorney to represent him, or the defendant may appear in pro per.

After the complaint is filed and served by the plaintiff, and answered by the defendant, a trial date is set. In today's somewhat complex legal world with which civil litigation deals, the ultimate trial date may be several years after the original complaint is filed. During this interim, the parties attempt to determine precisely what transpired in leading up to and following the incident with which the lawsuit deals. This process is called the Discovery Process. Each party is allowed to file a series of written questions (interrogatories) that the other party must answer under oath. Each party may command witnesses, or parties to the lawsuit, to appear before a court reporter and, under oath, provide a sworn statement (a deposition) as to their knowledge of the circumstances.

In addition to the discovery process going on to determine the factual issues, there is also the opportunity to file motions with the court pertaining to specific items of the law which are felt to be advantageous to one party or the other. The motions can address very small, almost insignificant, issues dealing with trial procedure. They also may be so central to the underlying issues of the case as to call for an immediate determination by the judge to either dismiss the lawsuit in favor of the defendant, or rule in favor of the plaintiff as a matter of law, thus foregoing the necessity of a trial. Understandably, neither of these somewhat drastic results is successfully arrived at very often.

While the discovery phase, and the motion phase, are going on, thus moving the case toward disposition at trial, there is often activity by one or both parties to continue to try to resolve the matter without going to trial. While it was indicated earlier that only a very small percentage of cases wind up in the litigation process, an even smaller number are actually tried before a judge and jury. The vast majority of the cases are resolved by mutual agreement. In those situations, the claimant signs a release that discharges the defendant from any further claim being brought in the matter. The defendant pays the agreed upon amount (assuming it is a monetary settlement), and the lawsuit is dismissed.

In the few cases that cannot be resolved via a mutually agreeable settlement, the case is ultimately assigned to a judge for trial. Either party has the right to request a jury trial, however, if neither party makes that request the case will be held before, and ruled upon, by the judge. This is called a Bench Trial. In jury trials, it is the jury's function to consider all matters of fact, while the judge is responsible for ruling on all matters of law. In a bench trial, the judge will rule on both matters of law and matters of fact.

In jury trials, prospective jurors are called and each party, along with the judge, asks a series of questions to determine if the prospective juror has any bias or prejudice which would render that individual unable to provide a fair and impartial verdict. This is called *voir dire*, from the Latin meaning to speak the truth. If a juror is found to have such bias or prejudice, the juror may be dismissed "for cause." Each side generally has an unlimited number of challenges to jurors for cause, so long as the judge agrees the cause is reasonable.

In addition to dismissing a juror for cause, each side usually has a limited number (determined by the local court system and/or the State or Federal court having jurisdiction over the matter) of "peremptory challenges" against prospective jurors. There is no requirement to indicate why the prospective juror is being dismissed, and until the peremptory challenges are exhausted, either party may rule out any prospective juror. The number of jurors and alternates is determined by the rules of the court hearing the matter.

When a full jury is impaneled, the trial begins with each party (or their legal representative) making an opening statement to the jury. It is here that the case to be presented by both parties is laid out for the jury to hear. The parties will indicate what they intend to prove, and will outline for the jury, certain matters they deem to be important.

During the trial each side is allowed to call witnesses to testify before the jury. The witnesses generally are the same group of people who were deposed during the discovery stage of the pretrial activity. When one side calls a witness to testify, the other side then is allowed to cross-examine the witness on testimony given. When the opposing side finishes their cross examination, the side which called the witness may reexamine the witness to attempt to correct any confusion or miscommunication given by the witness.

In some cases, expert witnesses are called to testify for one or both sides. Experts are people who possess certain specific knowledge of aspects in question in the trial, and whom the court agrees will shed additional light on certain subjects to benefit the jury in their quest for a verdict.

After all witnesses have been heard and evidence introduced, each side again gets to address the jury. This is called the Summation or Closing Arguments. This time, the parties sum up what they have introduced and what certain witnesses said. The jury is asked to consider certain items and to disregard others. Each side attempts to win the jury to their position.

When the parties or their lawyers have completed their final arguments, the judge then provides the jury with specific instructions on the law. This is often called the Jury Charge or the Charge to the Jury. Since the jury is made up of laymen, generally unschooled in legal matters, they are not expected to know the law regarding the case at hand. The judge, at this time, informs the jurors as to what they must do under the law, and what they cannot do under the law. He advises them that if they find certain things to be true, a particular verdict must be brought back, while other findings on their part must result in some other verdict being rendered. Although these instructions are delivered by the judge in open court to the jury members, they are usually the product of an earlier arrived at agreement between the judge and the lawyers trying the case.

After this "charge" to the jury, the jurors are taken to a jury deliberation room to consider what they have heard, and determine what they wish to do in the way of rendering a verdict. Although in a criminal trial the defendant is protected by the issue of reasonable doubt, no such legal restrictions apply in civil matters. The jurors are allowed to believe any portion of what they heard as testimony, and to disregard any or all other testimony. They may accept evidence, or disregard it. They are allowed to accept the "preponderance of the evidence", which means they are able to accept what they believe to be true based on what they heard as jurors. They cannot use their own personal knowledge or backgrounds, or rely on anything other than what they heard or saw in the courtroom. Also unlike a criminal trial, the jury's verdict need not be unanimous. A simple majority is all that is required in most jurisdictions.

When the jury has decided on the issues of liability, and (if appropriate) damages, they return to the courtroom and their verdict is announced. The trial phase, except in very few circumstances, is completed at this point. That does not mean, however, that the matter is finalized.

The party that did not prevail may ask the court to throw out the verdict, thus ignoring the jury's deliberations and decision. This is a "verdict N.O.V." (*non obstante verdicto*.) While possible, this is rarely done. Either party can also ask the judge to change the amount of the damages assessed by the jury's verdict. The plaintiff may feel the evidence and the verdict were incompatible, and that a finding in their favor should have resulted in a higher damages award. This would be asking the judge for an Additur. Likewise, the defendant against whom the verdict has been rendered may feel the damage assessment was too high, given the evidence presented. They may ask the judge for a Remittitur, thus reducing the amount of damages associated with the verdict.

After a verdict is rendered, and officially entered by the court, thus making it binding, either party has the right to appeal to a higher court, so long as there are some issues that allow such action. That is to say, it is not sufficient to merely be unhappy with the outcome of the lower court proceedings. There must be some issue of law on which the side seeking the appeal can base their plea for further redress. With the complexities of the law today, and the civil court proceedings, it is a rarity to be unable to find some point that cannot be argued as an appealable issue.

The appellate process is somewhat different from the lower court proceedings. Generally speaking, the appeals courts are presented with written documents (called briefs — which are usually anything but brief) prepared by the parties and setting forth the issues that the appeals court is asked to decide. Witnesses are almost never heard at this level. The appeals court can affirm the lower court decision, thus telling the appealing party the verdict was correct; or they can overturn the lower court decision and render a different verdict; or they can find an error in the lower court trial and remand the case back to the previous court to be tried again in light of the appeals court ruling on the legal issue presented.

Beyond the appeal to the appellate courts, the parties may ask the State Supreme Court, or the United States Supreme Court to review the case; however, in order to reach these levels it is necessary to have a question of a constitutional issue, rather than merely a matter of legislative or common law.

Arbitration and/or Mediation:

At times, and under certain circumstances, it is possible to resolve differences related to a claim by use of a forum other than the courts. One alternative dispute resolution method is Arbitration. Since this form of resolution process is generally less formal than is the court system, almost any type of ground rules are possible, so long as they are agreeable to all parties. Nevertheless, the American Arbitration Association (AAA) has established guidelines for many of the possible procedures, and most parties agree to be bound by the rules and procedures established by the AAA.

A second similar method of dispute resolution is Mediation. This method is also used to resolve disputes, by agreement, without resorting to litigation and normal court proceedings. Instead, the matter is resolved by appointed, or agreed upon, individuals to hear evidence and render a decision.

Arbitration and mediation may be either Binding or Non-Binding. Binding Arbitration or Mediation will commit all parties to accept the decision of the arbitration or mediation panel, and no further action can be taken to pursue or resist the claim. The arbitration or mediation decision will resolve the matter at that point.

If the arbitration or mediation is non-binding, then either party may choose to ignore any or all of the findings. While this may not resolve the entire matter, even non-binding arbitration or mediation can show each side the possible weaknesses in their respective positions, and very often will lead to some negotiated resolution, usually based loosely on the arbitration/mediation findings.

While the litigation process is commenced via the use of the Summons and Complaint process, arbitration and/or mediation is usually initiated by one party or the other merely giving notice of its intent to follow this route.

The availability of these alternative processes often emanates from a contractual clause contained in some type of previously signed agreement between the parties. Such a pre-arranged agreement to arbitrate or mediate is not, however, necessary. Even in the absence of such a contract clause or other earlier agreement, the parties may still decide to settle their differences by arbitration or mediation, rather than the courts, merely by agreeing to do so.

The advantages of arbitration and mediation are that they are usually much faster than is the court process, and as a result are usually also substantially less expensive. Either party can be represented by an attorney, just as with litigated proceedings, and there may be the opportunity to conduct much of the same type of pretrial discovery that was discussed above dealing with court litigation.

The arbitration or mediation process between the parties is usually accomplished by one party selecting an arbitrator/mediator, and the other party selecting a second similar individual. Those two selected representatives then agree on a third person. As indicated, there is much greater latitude in these types of proceedings, and if both parties agree, a single arbitrator or mediator may be selected to hear the case.

The arbitrators or mediators examine the facts submitted by each side and resolve whatever points are in contention. While the arbitration and mediation processes may be less structured than court proceedings, there will generally still be some type of formal hearing with the arbitrators or mediators acting as judge and jury. Witnesses may be called, evidence may be submitted, and the parties may have the opportunity to present oral arguments in favor of their position.

State Workers' Compensation Hearings:

With the passage of Workers' Compensation laws by the various states throughout America, employees were given certain rights beyond those granted to the general public. (See Chapter 1.) When an employee is injured during the course and scope of employment, the claim for medical payments, lost wages, disability, etc., is handled by a state agency. Disputes between the employee and employer (or the employer's insurance carrier) are not resolved in the courts via civil litigation or arbitration, but by specially empowered judges, arbitrators, referees, or panels.

When an injured worker is unable to receive what he considers to be the proper amount or degree of restitution called for under the Workers' Compensation laws of the jurisdiction having control of his claim, the injured worker is allowed to file a claim with the appropriate state board or commission which has been created for such matters.

Since Workers' Compensation laws are matters of legislative enactments by individual states, the methods for adjudicating disputes varies from state to state. Nevertheless, there are many similarities, and general programs in existence from state to state. (See Chapter 12.)

If an injured worker and his employer (via the employer's Workers' Compensation insurer) are unable to resolve a dispute relating to any of the various aspects of Workers' Compensation benefits, the employee may file a claim with the appropriate state agency. There is usually no requirement for the worker to be represented by an attorney in these matters, however the vast majority of claimants in this situation do seek legal counsel.

The same legislation that grants various rights to workers who are injured on the job, also provides the employer with certain safeguards that would not otherwise be available under common law. Although the requirement to prove negligence is removed, the injured worker must forgo such things as "pain and suffering" (a common and often expensive item of damages in civil litigation.)

Once the claim has been filed with the W.C. Board or Commission, a hearing is set for the introduction of testimony and evidence. The injured worker may submit medical reports or other evidence to dispute the medical findings of the treating physician, if those findings are being challenged. Similarly, the issues of disability, or dependents (where that is pertinent), or the facts of the accident that caused the injury can all be examined at the Workers' Compensation hearing.

In most jurisdictions, the primary hearing is held before a single judge, commissioner, arbitrator, referee, or other properly designated trier of the facts. A decision is then rendered as to the questions raised in the initial filing of the claim. In few jurisdictions, if any, is the hearing officer's finding the final word on the matter. The decision may be appealed to the next highest level within the Workers' Compensation system, either a panel of similar judges or commissioners, and/or — in certain circumstances — to the civil courts.

The vehicle by which a Workers' Compensation claim finds it's way into the civil courts is by way of a Writ of Certiorari. This is an order from the appropriate civil court to the Workers' Compensation venue that heard the case, in effect ordering the case into civil court for a hearing to determine if the Workers' Compensation ruling was proper and accurate. In the event the matter does find its way to the courts, the case is treated — from the standpoint of litigation procedure — much as any other lawsuit filed in that legal jurisdiction. However, it is still subject to the requirements and protections written into the Workers' Compensation laws by the legislature.

There are certain Federal statutes that govern Workers' Compensation laws pertaining to employees of the United States government. These laws are generally administered by the United States Department of Labor, which will hold hearings on disputed Workers' Compensation claims of Federal employees in much the same manner as do state W.C. boards or commissions adjudicating the claims of employees of private companies.

Workers' Compensation jurisdiction under the United States Department of Labor also extends to certain injured parties not employed by the Federal government, but otherwise coming under the U.S.D.L. protections. These include such groups as civilian employees, working on government military bases or under government contracts, who would be covered under the Federal Defense Base Act. The U.S.D.L. would also cover employees of private shipping companies who are injured while in United States navigable waters, and longshoreman or harbor workers doing certain stevedoring chores. Such injured workers would be covered by the United States Longshoremen's and Harbor Worker's Act.

Chapter Six

Insurance Premium

The charge that an insurance company assesses when it agrees to assume part or all of a risk is called premium. The premium is meant to cover the anticipated losses associated with the policy coverage, plus expenses, and a reasonable profit. This does not always turn out to be the case.

Obviously, since insurance deals with what might occur in the future, it is impossible to predict precisely what the losses will be. To enable them to come closer in their projections, insurance companies use actuaries who look at past trends and patterns, and make predictions as to what will happen in the future. (See Chapter 3). The actuarial calculations are based on statistics from other similar kinds of policies and the losses sustained under those policies. In its purest sense, the proper amount of a premium assessment is the amount the insurance company will pay for all losses sustained by the insured, plus outside expenses related to the insurance, plus internal costs such as salaries, etc., plus a reasonable profit. That type of formula, however, is not actually used for most premium calculations.

On any given individual insurance policy, the probabilities of being correct in the assumptions about future losses is very low; however, the insurance industry uses what is called "The Law of Large Numbers." What this means is that with a large enough group of policies, they are able to predict with some accuracy that a certain percentage will suffer certain types of losses. While they cannot guess as to which specific policy may encounter the loss, by insuring large groups they can spread their risk so they will have sufficient premium from the policies that do not sustain a loss, to cover those that do.

For many types of insurance, the various Departments of Insurance in the states where the policies will be sold regulate the premium charges. The insurance department's attempt to control the premium amounts that may be charged is an effort to assist the insurance buying public, and to guard against companies developing a monopolistic type of price fixing. In effect, most states themselves do the price fixing by regulating what a company can charge as premium for a specific type of policy.

In the early days of insurance, there was much more speculation required on loss frequency and severity. As the industry matured and prospered, formulas and patterns were developed to enable the underwriters to assign classifications to certain groups. For these risk classifications, a basic premium is calculated. The underwriter may then add additional charges to increase the premium on a specific policy so as to reflect a risk greater than the norm of the general class; or offer credits to reduce the premium for a risk in the class that has below average risk potential.

Insurance companies desiring to conduct business in a particular state must file certain information on what types of coverage they will be providing, and the premium levels they will charge. It is quite possible that some companies will willingly charge less than the amount approved by the state Department of Insurance, in order to capture a larger share of the market. It is also possible that a given company may be able to obtain approval from the state to charge more than some other company for substantially the same coverage. A company cannot, however, merely decide unilaterally to increase their premium charges. They must petition the state to increase their fees. The justification for such increases is usually accomplished by showing extraordinary claims costs, and/or higher than normal expenses. When this occurs over a number of years, an insurance department may grant a carrier the right to increase their premium fees.

If the fee increase is requested and granted to a number of companies, the rates in that state go up and the insurance companies continue to forage for their respective shares of the available insureds. If the rate increase is brought about because an individual company is unable to function at the current rate structure, while other companies seem to be functioning within the standard parameter, the company receiving the right to raise their rates may well be unable to compete with the other carriers who continue to charge a lower rate.

State insurance departments do not want insurance companies to go out of business or to withdraw from their state's markets, since that decreases the number of insurers for selection by residents of the state. At the same time, the insurance departments have a built in need to attempt to maintain the pricing structure at reasonable and existing rates to provide insureds in their states with affordable insurance.

Most states require that every insurance company writing business in their state contribute to some sort of a Guarantee Fund, which is organized to meet the financial obligations of any insurer that becomes insolvent and is unable to pay their loses. Although the state insurance departments attempt to keep close watch over the dealings of insurers operating within their states, periodically an insurance company is unable to continue to do business and these Guarantee Funds allow the policy holders and the general public to obtain at least a portion of the claim payment they might have been owed from the now insolvent insurer.

Premium rates may differ widely from state to state and can even show vast differences from one area of a state to another in that same state. The same rational as is discussed above generally holds true whether the rates are being regulated for a given state, or for specific locales within a state.

Earlier in this chapter it was noted that an insurance company must be licensed in a particular state in order to do business in that state. An exception to this general rule is what is known as Non-Admitted Insurance Companies. A company that is fully licensed in a state, and therefore allowed to write business for which it has been granted such permission, is an Admitted Carrier. These companies may sell directly to the insureds via their own sales force, or they may offer their products through a network of agents and brokers who market and sell the policies for them. (See Chapter 3.)

Some insurance companies may not be fully licensed to do business in a particular state, but are nevertheless allowed to provide their policies under certain specific situations. These are called Non-Admitted Carriers. Under most circumstances, a policy cannot be written by a non-admitted carrier unless the same coverage is unavailable from admitted carriers, or highly restricted in the scope of the coverage being offered by the admitted carriers.

When a prospective insured is unable to find an admitted carrier in his state who can offer the type of coverage desired, the business may be placed with a non-admitted carrier. While non-admitted carriers are not subject to the same degree of scrutiny as are admitted carriers, the state departments of insurance nevertheless still control much of the non-admitted carriers activities and actions.

The premium ultimately charged by an insurance company — admitted or non-admitted — very often does not include any specific profit ingredient. In fact, many times the cost to the insurance company, for losses plus expenses, exceeds the premium charged. This does not mean, however, that in the long run the insurer is actually operating at a loss.

Unlike the cost for most other goods and services, charges for insurance protection (premium) are usually paid in advance. Insurance premiums are charged for the entire policy period, and are payable when the policy goes into effect. This is actually a form of prepayment whereby the insurance company receives money for services (protection) to be rendered in the future. As a result, insurers have large funds of capital from the premiums collected that they are able to invest.

A policy written for a one year period will usually have an annual premium that is fully owed when the coverage goes into effect, even though the protection that is being purchased will actually accrue one day at a time over the life of the policy. As a result, the insurance company has the use of the premium payment for the entire time the policy is in effect. This "pot" of money is, of course, invested by the insurer, and the investment profit is a crucial ingredient in the insurer's bottom line profit margin. This investment profit, however, is not one of the ingredients that is usually considered in establishing premium rates. Therefore, a carrier, anticipating this investment income, might charge rates that will actually produce income less than the losses plus expenses.

Depending on the investment climate at any given time, the profits gained by the insurance companies from these investments can add large gains to their bottom line profitability.

The amount of premium that an insurance company charges

for a policy, or a group of policies, is called the Written Premium. This is the gross premium figure. Since the premiums are charged in advance, the company has not actually earned the premium until they perform the services to which they agreed in the policy; that is, to provide protection as indicated in the Insuring Agreement.

In other words, the day the policy takes effect, the entire premium cost is the written premium. The earned premium would be zero, since nothing would have yet been earned. The unearned premium would be the same amount as the written premium, since the entire policy period would still be ahead. After the first day (on a one year policy), 1/365 of the written premium would be earned, and 364/365 would be unearned. On day two, earned premium would be 2/365, and the unearned would be 363/365. This is admittedly an over simplification, but should provide a better understanding of these terms and how they relate to one another.

Not all premiums are assessed at the inception of a policy. Some policies are written with what is called a Retro-Premium. In such cases, there is usually a portion of the anticipated premium that is charged "up front", as with all other policies; however, the policy is then reassessed at the end of the policy term and the premium is adjusted. This means the insurance company may be entitled to additional premium, or may be required to return some of the premium to the insured.

Retro-premium accounts are usually large and complex insureds where determining the scope of the future losses is very difficult. In some cases, the amount of the premium may be tied to the amount of sales the insured will have during the policy period, or to the amount of their payroll reflecting the size of their work force, or to any other factor that may vary during the policy term.

Instead of paying the entire premium at the inception of the policy, the insured and the carrier agree that the insurance will be provided, and the insured will reimburse the company for all losses, all expenses, and a reasonable profit. In these cases, the insurance company is not able to use the entire premium for investment purposes, since the majority of the premium will not be paid until the policy expires. On the other hand, the carrier is often guaranteed a profit in the retro-premium calculations.

Insurance companies are required to set aside certain amounts of money to cover their anticipated losses. Out of the total amount of premiums the company collects from its policyholders they must establish a monetary "loss reserve" for each claim reported. This is the claims handler's best estimate of the cost to settle the loss. In addition, an amount must also be established to cover the cost of the direct expenses related to the claim, such as adjustment expenses, legal expenses, etc. These claims expenses are "Allocated Loss Adjustment Expenses" (ALAE).

In addition to the direct expenses (ALAE) that are anticipated and can be allocated to a particular policy, there are other expenses that will be incurred but which do not related directly to an individual policy. These "Unallocated Loss Adjustment Expenses" (ULAE) include such things as employee salaries, transportation allowances, training costs, etc.

Finally, the reserves must include an additional factor to cover claims that history has told us have probably already happened (incurred), but which have not yet come to the attention of the insurance company. These claims are referred to as "incurred but not reported" (IBNR). The amounts set aside for these IBNR reserves are established by actuaries who develop models of future loss frequency based on past loss history.

The remainder of the total premiums collected, after all these mandatory reserves are set aside, is the "surplus", or "underwriting surplus", of the company. Understandably, the surplus fluctuates almost constantly; however, with a large enough base — number of claims, gross written premium, etc. — the fluctuations are flattened somewhat and a general surplus can be calculated which remains relatively constant.

The underwriting surplus is an important calculation for an insurance company, since the amount of new premium they will be able to write is somewhat determined by the amount of this surplus. Financial organizations which rate insurance companies as to their financial stability and their ability to pay anticipated claims (such as Best's Rating Systems), carefully watch the ratio between the amount of premium any company writes and the amount of surplus held by that company. If a company is writing new premiums at a rate of two or three times their surplus, it is generally considered sound business. If a carrier writes five, or six, or seven times it's surplus, most state insurance departments would be concerned that their writings were too large to be reasonably covered by the carrier's assets. The financial rating bureaus that monitor the carriers also become concerned when an insurance company's writings grow too large in comparison to their existing policyholder s' surplus.

PART II
Specific Coverages

Chapter Seven

The Automobile Insurance Policy

The Automobile Insurance Policy, whether personal or commercial, generally covers several specific types of claims that the owner and/or operator may encounter. Occasionally, there are differences between the coverage or language in a personal auto policy and a commercial policy. Those differences will be pointed out as they are discussed in this chapter.

The auto policy can be viewed as if it is several policies in one. The coverages generally found in the auto policy include (1) Liability Coverage, covering bodily injury and/or property damage claims of others, brought against the insured; (2) Physical Damage Coverage, covering damage to the vehicle(s) owned or operated by the insured; (3) Medical Payments Coverage, providing for payment of medical expenses to people injured by the insured vehicle, or those operating, riding in, or being in contact with an insured vehicle when injured; and (4) Uninsured or Underinsured Motorist Coverage, which will provide for payments for injury or damage to insureds who are involved in an accident with someone who does not carry automobile insurance, or whose automobile insurance covers only a limited amount of the resultant costs.

Since the auto policy is actually several policies in one, each covering the aspects of operating a motor vehicle as outlined above, the policy itself often does not conform completely to the general format discussed in Chapter 4, "The Basic Policy Format." That is to say, while the items discussed in Chapter 4 are contained in the automobile policy form, they are, at times, merely located in a somewhat different part of the policy.

As with most other policies, the Declarations Page of the automobile policy is usually found at the front of the policy form, and generally contains all of the information discussed in the Declarations Page section of Chapter 4. In addition to the identification and address of the named insured, any Loss Payee(s), the types of coverage being provided, and the types of any specific endorsements, the Declarations Page will also identify the vehicle(s) being insured under the policy. In a commercial policy, in which multiple types and kinds of vehicles are being insured under the policy, the vehicle identification will usually be contained in a special endorsement to the policy, rather than on the Declarations Page. If the commercial vehicles insured under the policy are replaced, and others added, the endorsement is amended without need to reissue a new Declarations Page or a new policy.

This uniformity of format for the location of the Insuring Agreements, the Conditions, and the Exclusions, discussed in Chapter 4 relating to policies in general, is often less obvious in the auto policies. In many cases, the auto policy will incorporate, within the specific section of the policy, the insuring language, conditions, and exclusions that are applicable to that specific coverage. For instance, the section of the policy covering Liability will have the applicable terms and conditions contained in the Liability Section, rather than in a neatly labeled portion of the policy containing the Conditions, etc., for the entire policy. Similarly, the section dealing with Physical Damage will have the terms and conditions relating to that coverage contained in the Physical Damage section, and so forth. Certain conditions or definitions that apply to the policy as a whole, or to all sections equally, may be found in a General Provisions section.

Part 1 of the policy, the Liability Section, provides Coverage A for Bodily Injury, and Coverage B for Property Damage. The insuring agreement language in this section may say something like:

> *"The company agrees to pay all sums for which the insured may become legally liable because of bodily injury or property damage caused by an occurrence, arising out of the ownership, maintenance or use of an automobile or other vehicle insured under this part."*

> *"The company will defend any suit claiming damages for bodily injury or property damage if covered by this policy, even if the allegations of the lawsuit are groundless, false or fraudulent."*

There is usually a clause in this area that discusses Additional Payments. This includes the acknowledgement that the company will also pay for (1) their own costs in investigating, defending and paying for any claim under the policy, (2) payment of interest on judgments rendered against the insured, (3) payment of appeal bond premiums if a judgment is appealed, or for bonds related to an arrest for a traffic violation arising under this part of the policy,

(4) payment of reasonable expenses incurred by the insured for any loss occasioned by the insured's required presence at a hearing, trial, etc., and (5) expenses an insured may incur for emergency first aid in assisting someone involved in an accident covered under this section of the policy.

The persons insured under the Liability Section usually include the named insured, whose name appears on the Declarations Page, any person using the insured vehicle with the permission of the owner or any other named insured, and in the Personal Automobile Policy, any relative living with the named insured. In Commercial Automobile policies, the definition of the term "insured" may include the officers and employees of the named insured.

The coverage provided under the Liability Section of the automobile policy may, in certain circumstances, apply to the insured's operation of a vehicle other than that which is owned by him or which is identified in the policy, such as a rented or borrowed automobile. There may be wording in the policy to further limit the definition of who is insured under such circumstances.

In the Liability Section of the automobile policy, definitions will usually be found for automobile, insured automobile, private passenger automobile, utility automobile, substitute automobile, occurrence, relative, use of an automobile, and many others.

There may also be specific exclusions outlined here which are applicable only to the Liability Section. Some generally excluded circumstances include use of the vehicle for livery purposes, damage resulting from intentional acts by the insured, injury to employees of the insured, injuries covered under a Workers' Compensation insurance policy, and damage to property which is in the insured's care, custody or control.

It is important to note that the use of an automobile under a personal automobile insurance policy is not limited to only personal use. Unless the policy is endorsed with a specific exclusion prohibiting the vehicle from commercial usage, the car can be driven for business purposes with full coverage. There is generally no "business pursuits" exclusion as might be found in some other kinds of personal insurance policies such as the Homeowner's policy.

Because the automobile policy is really several policies bound together by their commonality of purpose and scope, the Limits of Liability will be different for the various coverages found in the policy. The specific dollar Limits of Liability for each section are usually spelled out in the Declarations Page; however, the conditions relating to the Limits for each section may be contained in the specific wording of that section.

The Declarations Page will set forth the maximum amount the insurer will pay to any one individual in any single accident or occurrence, and the total amount the insurer will pay in any one accident or occurrence regardless of how many individual claimants are involved. These two amounts may be different (a split limits policy) or the same (a single limit policy). The amounts may be broken down between the amounts payable for bodily injury and for property damage, or the two types of payments may also be lumped into a single limit. The insurer may indicate an annual aggregate limit that sets forth the total amount they will pay for all accidents under the policy during the time the coverage is in effect, or the policy may be silent on this topic. Any specific details related to the Limits of Liability that are unique to the Liability Section will generally be included in the Liability Section itself.

Although it is possible to have a deductible applying to the coverages under the Liability Section of the policy, it is somewhat rare. If such a deductible were contained, it would generally be indicated on the Declarations Page, and would be contained in a specifically worded endorsement attached to the policy.

Part 2 of the policy, Medical Payments, provides coverage for the payment of medical and funeral expenses incurred by certain individuals due to bodily injury while operating a motor vehicle or if struck by a motor vehicle, as well as to others who might be operating, using, or riding in a vehicle insured under the policy.

Unlike the Liability section of the policy, which pays damages for which the insured may be legal liable, the medical payments section of the policy will pay medical bills regardless of fault or legal liability.

Once again, there may be definitions or conditions that apply specifically to this section of the policy, and those specific definitions will be found in the Medical Payments section.

The Limit of Liability for this section is generally specified in the Declarations Page, but may be otherwise restricted or modified by language contained in the specific Medical Payments section.

Since the Medical Payments coverage is a "first party" benefit, and one in which the insurance company is agreeing to pay benefits for damages possibly caused by some other party, the insurer can retain the right to proceed against the at-fault party to recoup their payment. This is a right that the insured would have by law. It is, therefore, necessary that the right be conveyed to the insurance company. The insurance company may proceed against the wrongdoer in their own name, on behalf of their insured, or jointly with the insured. This process is called Subrogation and is further discussed in Chapter 5, "Legal Issues."

In some circumstances, the insured may elect to accept payment for the medical bills from their own carrier under the Medical Payment section, and to also seek damages (including those same medical bills) from the party who caused the accident. It is their right to do so; however, the Medical Payments section may have wording to the effect that if the insured collects from the other party, they must reimburse their own carrier for what was paid under the Medical Payments section.

As with the Liability section, a deductible provision referable to

Medical Payments coverage is possible, but rare. If one exists, it would be indicated on the Declarations Page, and would be represented by a specifically worded endorsement attached to the policy.

In Part 3 of the policy, coverage is provided for Physical Damage to the insured vehicle(s). This should not be confused with the property damage coverage contained in Part 1 of the policy. In Part 1, the coverage was for damage to the property of someone else. Part 3 provides for the payment of damages to the insured vehicle(s).

The coverage in this section of the policy is usually contained in two or more sub-sections. One portion deals with Collision Coverage. Collision Coverage pertains to damage to the insured vehicle that was caused by contact between the insured vehicle and another object, or from the vehicle overturning. A second coverage provided in this section is Comprehensive Coverage, and is usually defined to mean loss from other than collision. This comprehensive coverage usually includes such things as damage caused by missiles, falling objects, fire, theft, explosion, earthquake, windstorm, hail, water, flood, malicious mischief, riot or civil commotion. Glass breakage is generally included, but may be dealt with somewhat differently than the other perils.

A deductible is almost always contained in the Collision Coverage Section. It is less universally found applying to the Comprehensive Coverage, but this has become more prevalent in the last decade or so. The deductible is often waived on glass breakage claims, even if a collision and/or comprehensive deductible are present. The specific information pertaining to deductibles in this section of the policy will be found in the Declarations Page.

Part 3 of the policy often contains a provision whereby the insurer will reimburse the insured for the cost of a rental vehicle, following an accident covered by the policy, if the insured vehicle is rendered undriveable, or if the vehicle is out of use due to repairs being made.

There may be specific restrictions or other limiting considerations such as a daily maximum rental charge, all of which will be spelled out in this section of the policy.

The maximum an insurance company will generally pay for the repair or replacement of an insured vehicle is the actual cash value of the vehicle at the time of the accident. If the vehicle is declared a total loss; i.e., the damages exceed the value of the vehicle, and the insurance company pays their insured that value, the vehicle generally then belongs to the carrier (although this may be negotiated between the parties on a case by case basis). If the carrier takes possession of the totaled vehicle, they will generally sell it as salvage to recoup a portion of their loss.

This coverage is also a "first party" coverage, and if the insured elects to collect from their own insurance company, the insurer will demand the right to pursue anyone who caused the damages. This is called Subrogation (See Chapter 5, "Legal Issues"), and will usually be found in the Automobile Physical Damage section of the policy.

As with the other sections of the policy, there may be specific exclusions or definitions that pertain primarily or exclusively to the Part 3 coverages, and these will be found in this section of the policy. Similarly, the Limits of Liability are substantially different for this section than for some other sections such as the Liability Section.

In Part 4 of the policy, coverage is provided for Uninsured Motorist Coverage and/or Underinsured Motorist Coverage. Since some people opt to drive without automobile insurance protection, or because some circumstances might invalidate the insurance protection of a person who causes an accident, the general public is allowed to purchase insurance coverage that will protect them if damaged by a driver with no insurance, or with limited insurance protection.

This type of insurance functions as if your own insurance company was the insurer for the driver who was uninsured, or underinsured, and caused your damage. The insured may make claim under their own policy for much of the same type damage — bodily injury, property damage, mental stress, pain and suffering — as they would file against the other driver if that driver had been insured. Although some policies allow the insured to select a Limit of Liability for this type of coverage, very often the Limit of Liability under the Uninsured or Underinsured Motorist Coverages is equal to the amount the insured carries for their own Liability Coverage in Part 1 of the policy.

This section will again indicate who may present a claim under this coverage, and will define certain pertinent items that have significance under the coverage.

Since this coverage is also a "first party" coverage, between the insurer and the insured, the policy usually contains a subrogation clause allowing the insurer to seek recovery of what they pay under this coverage directly from the uninsured or underinsured party. (See Chapter 5, "Legal Issues" for further discussion of Subrogation.)

Although the right to have legal issues of liability and damages resolved by a court of law would normally exist for the insured, that right is usually waived in the policy as between the insured and the insurance company. If there are unresolved issues between these two parties, the policy will often require the dispute be resolved by arbitration rather than by the courts.

A notable exception to this is in the case of an insurer denying coverage for part or all of a policy when presented with a claim. If the insured feels the coverage is being incorrectly or wrongly denied, they would have the right to bring suit against the insurer under a theory of "Bad Faith." The action would emanate from a contractual dispute between the parties, and in all contracts there is said to be a "Covenant of Good Faith and Fair Dealing" between the parties. Therefore, the action against the insurer would be allowed regardless of the policy language.

One of the most often referred to policy conditions is the Other Insurance Clause. In Chapter 4 of this text, the various types of Other Insurance Clauses are discussed, as are the ramifications of each when more than one insurance policy may be in effect.

Some policies will contain an Other Insurance Clause that applies to all sections of the policy, while others may have differing Other Insurance Clauses, each applying to a particular section of the policy. Usually, the various sections of the automobile policy will each contain their own Other Insurance Clause.

Any of the individual coverages that go into making up a "complete" automobile policy may be purchased by the insured, or declined. There is no requirement that one coverage be obtained if another is selected; however, it is rare, if not unheard of, to find a policy with Uninsured Motorist Coverage, or Medical Payments Coverage, without Liability Coverage. Liability coverage, on the other hand, is regularly written without the other coverages, especially where the vehicle is of marginal value and does not justify the cost of premiums for Physical Damage Coverage. Many policies are purchased with Liability and perhaps Physical Damage Coverage, but without the Medical Payments Coverage and/or the Uninsured Motorist Protection.

CHAPTER EIGHT

The Homeowner's Policy

T he Homeowner's Insurance Policy is actually the amalgamation of two policies — one protecting the structure (dwelling) and the personal property, etc., from specific and certain general hazards. This is known as "first party "coverage.

The second policy within the policy is the liability coverage portion that protects the homeowner (and certain others) from personal liability against claims for damages caused by the insured. This is referred to as "third party" coverage.

As with most other policies, the Declaration Page will set forth the insured's name, the residence location, policy period, coverages, limits of liability for the various coverages, and deductibles that might apply to certain coverages.

In Section I of the H.O. policy, "Coverage A" provides coverage for the principal residence, and includes the dwelling itself, any structures attached to the dwelling, structures not attached but forming part of the overall realty of the property, materials on the location used for construction, renovation, alterations, etc., foundations and footings that support the dwelling, and wall-to-wall carpeting attached to the dwelling. (Note that while some of these items might otherwise be considered "personal property" of the homeowner, they are usually included as part of the dwelling.)

The property under Coverage A is generally covered for all direct physical loss except for certain specific excluded items. These excluded areas under Coverage A include such things as the land itself, costs to restore or replace the land, and the costs of techniques designed to compensate or prevent land instability.

Unlike the Coverage A protection, the coverage under Coverage B (Personal Property) is generally "named perils"; i.e., rather than broadly encompassing most causes of loss (less some specific exceptions), the coverage for "B" is usually specific as to certain types of causation.

The types of loss that are protected against for Personal Property include such things as fire, lightning, wind, hail, explosion, riot or civil commotion, smoke, vandalism, theft, falling objects, weight of ice, snow or sleet, discharge or overflow of water or steam systems, freezing, glass breakage, and damages caused by aircraft, vehicles, or from artificially generated electrical current. (Some insurers do offer "All Risk" coverage. This is somewhat of a misnomer. All Risk coverage does not specify the perils being insured against, but does still contain many of the exclusions found in the Named Peril policies.)

Other losses not generally covered under Section I, either Coverage A or B, include certain damage to the dwelling if it is vacant at the time of loss; theft if the dwelling is under construction; continuous or repeated seepage of water or steam; wear, tear, marring, deterioration, inherent vice, latent defect or mechanical breakdown;

corrosion; mold; contamination; smog; vermin, rodents, insects or domestic animals; pressure from roots; earthquake, or nuclear hazard; enforcement of any ordinance or law; earth movement; water damage from surface water, or sewage from outside the premises; neglect, or war. There may be other exclusions in any given H.O. policy, and the specific form should be read in its entirety for a true and complete interpretation of the coverages and exclusions contained.

Settlements of claims for damage under Section I (Coverage A and B) are generally calculated at "replacement cost." That is to say that damages covered under this section of the policy are usually paid without consideration of depreciation. (Betterment may be considered in the settlement equation if the repairs constitute a substantial improvement in the value of the damaged property.)

In order to recoup the replacement cost of the damaged items, the repair or replacement must be completed. Often the carrier will pay the actual cash value of the damaged, destroyed or missing items following the loss, and will then make a supplemental payment for the increased value of the replacement cost when the repairs or replacement are complete.

Under Coverage B, the replacement cost aspect is often excluded on some items which, by their nature cannot be replaced or whose value is such that age, history, etc., have materially contributed to their value.

As with other insurance policies, the Conditions Section of Section I of the Homeowner's Policy will provide certain pertinent aspects of the coverage being provided. The Conditions usually address such items as the insured's duties in the event of a loss, the ability and restrictions of the insured to bring a legal action against the insurer, the settlement of a part of a pair or set, the result of property abandonment, the invalidating of the policy in the event of a loss occurring from the insured's intentional act(s), and the "Other Insurance Clause", which is discussed in the Basic Policy

Format (See Chapter 4). There may be other pertinent conditions and restrictions contained in the Conditions Section of the particular policy under consideration. The policy at issue should be read in its entirety.

The coverages being provided in the "first party" sections of the Homeowner's Policy are often expanded and/or modified through the inclusion of specific endorsements. It is possible for the insured, prior to a loss occurring, to insure specific items for pre-determined amounts. This is called "scheduling" these items. The scheduled items will usually be covered for all types of loss, and, in the event of loss or damage, will be paid for up to the amount for which they are scheduled, regardless of their actual cash value or their replacement cost.

Since many homes have a mortgage that the owner is paying to a lender, the mortgage company is usually endorsed onto the policy as a "Loss Payee" through the use of an endorsement. This will insure that in the event of a loss to the dwelling, the lender will be protected up to the amount of their interest in the property. The Loss Payee will be identified by name on the Declarations Page.

Any endorsement may be made to the policy, so long as the insured and the carrier agree on what changes are being occasioned by the endorsement, and what, if any, premium impact the endorsement might have.

Section II of the Homeowner's Policy provides Personal Liability Insurance Protection to anyone insured under the policy. This section will pay for bodily injury and property damage, to which the coverage applies, if a claim or lawsuit is brought against anyone qualifying as an insured under the policy. It will also pay for a defense of the claim or lawsuit, and will provide the insurer the right (but generally not the obligation) to investigate any such claim or lawsuit.

The Personal Liability section also pays for first aid expenses incurred by the insured in providing necessary emergency treatment for bodily injury covered by the policy.

In addition to the Personal Liability protection found in Section II of the Homeowner's Policy, the standard form also includes Medical Payments Coverage. This should not be confused with the payment for injury sustained and covered under the Liability portion of the policy.

The Medical Payments Coverage is not predicated, as is the liability coverage, on the insured's legal liability. Rather, it provides payment regardless of legal fault for needed medical expenses to anyone (other than an insured) who is injured on the premises, or for an injury caused by the activities of an insured, a residence employee, or an animal owned by the insured. The Medical Payments Coverage may also pay medical costs sustained by a residence employee while working at the insured premises; however, there may be a Workers' Compensation exclusion in the policy that could negate such a payment to a domestic employee. (See below.)

There are exclusions pertaining to Section II (both the Liability and the Medical Payments protection.). These coverages do not pay for damages either expected or intended by the insured, or those that arise out of the insured's business pursuits. Bodily injury or property damage are not covered if they arise from the ownership, maintenance, use, loading or unloading of an aircraft, motor vehicle, or watercraft. The coverage is also excluded if the injuries or damages arise from war; from participation in an organized race or competition; or if they occur to anyone insured under the policy.

The Conditions referable to Section II of the policy indicate the insured's duties in the event of a loss, and usually contain a Severability Clause (See Glossary), as well as an Other Insurance Clause. (See Chapter 4, The Basic Policy, and the Glossary.)

In some states, and with some insurers, the Homeowner's Policy may also include a section providing coverage for Workers'

Compensation benefits for residence employees. The provisions contained in such a Homeowner's Policy section generally follow the state's requirements on coverage for Workers' Compensation. (See Chapter 14 covering the Commercial Workers' Compensation Policy.)

As with all other policy forms, it is necessary to read the entire policy for the type of coverage being reviewed.

CHAPTER NINE

The Standard Fire Policy

O ne of the early types of insurance policies provided to consumers was the Standard Fire Policy, sometimes referred to
as "the 165 line" fire policy. The format of this policy is somewhat
different than many of the forms that followed it, but it is still comprised of the parts discussed in Chapter 4, "The Basic Policy".

Seldom, if ever, will anyone any longer see the "165 line policy"
as a "stand-alone" form; however, many of the aspects contained
within this form were carried over to subsequent policy types. Also,
because of the impact this format had on the industry in earlier
times, no review of this subject would be complete without considering this policy structure.

Generally the first page of this policy comprises the Declaration,
with the insured's name, address, location of the building(s) being

insured, the limits of liability, the premium, etc.

In addition, this initial page often also includes what would be considered a partial Insuring Agreement, certain Exclusions, and many of the Conditions. Standard wording constituting the partial Insuring Agreement would be something to the effect that the policy insures against "... direct loss by fire, lightning and the removal of property from premises endangered by the perils insured against." As can be seen, this is a "named peril" policy, rather than an "all risk" policy as were later versions of many property-casualty insurance contracts.

Another difference between the Standard Fire Policy and some later policies insuring against loss to property (such as the Homeowners' Policy and the Commercial Package Policy) is that this policy is written on an ACV (Actual Cash Value) loss basis. That is, in the event of a loss, the damaged or destroyed property will not be settled based on what it would cost to replace the property, but rather what the value of the property is at the time of the loss. Depreciation, betterment, wear and tear, etc., would be calculated to determine the value of the damaged or destroyed property, up to the limits of liability. The policy calls for the repair, rebuilding, or replacement of the damaged property with "like kind and quality." This means the replacement, etc., is done with property valued on the same basis as was the destroyed or damaged property at the time of the loss. (See the Coverage section later in this chapter, and specifically that portion dealing with lines 141 through 147.)

Certain exclusions are mentioned on the first page of the Standard Fire Policy. Usually these policies exclude any allowance for increased repair costs by reason of local laws or ordinances regulating construction or repairs. This is important since certain such laws or ordinances may require added safety features or retro-fit requirements that are required at the time the repairs are made, but which were not in effect when the property was initially built or acquired. Although these added costs would be incurred in order to be in legal compliance when the repairs or replacements are made, those added costs would be the responsibility of the insured and not reimbursed by the carrier.

Similarly, the first page might contain an exclusion that the policy would not pay for added loss occasioned by interruption of business or manufacturing – a coverage (Business Interruption) often provided in later commercial property forms.

Some matters usually contained in the Conditions section of most policies can often be found on this first page of the Standard Fire Policy. One example might be the admonition that the policy cannot be assigned except by written consent of the insurer.

The second page of the Standard Fire Policy has 165 numbered lines (thus its pseudonym, "the 165 line fire policy.")

- Lines 1 – 6 indicates the policy will be voided in the event of concealment and/or fraud on the part of the insured.

- Lines 7 – 10 excludes certain property from being covered even if damaged or destroyed by a named peril. These uninsured items include such things as bills, currency, deeds, securities, etc.

- Lines 11 – 24 provides specific exclusions to the coverage. These are damages from, or occasioned by, (a) enemy attack, war, etc.; (b) invasion ;(c) insurrection; (d) rebellion; (e) revolution; (f) civil war; (g) usurped power; (h) order of civil authority; (i) neglect of the insured to save or protect the property; and (j) theft. (Note this last very important exclusion that is an integral part of the later property coverages such as the Homeowner's Policy.)

- Lines 25 – 27 is the Other Insurance Clause which, unlike the primary Other Insurance Clauses in subsequent policies (See Chapter 4, The Basic Policy Format), merely states that other insurance may be prohibited (exculpatory) or limited (pro-rated or primary) by endorsement to the policy. (Also see lines 86-89, discussed later in this chapter.)

- Lines 28 – 37 provides additional conditions suspending or restricting coverage (a) if the hazard is increased by the insured's knowledge or actions; (b) if the building otherwise covered is vacant; and (c) results from explosion or riot (except for any resultant fire damage, which is covered.)

- Lines 38 – 41 states that other perils may be added to the policy via endorsement(s).

- Lines 42 – 48 states that additional provisions may be added to the policy in writing, but no provisions may be waived unless allowed by the terms in the policy itself.

- Lines 49 – 55 reiterates the requirements that only written permission is valid to change the policy, and provides that the company will not waive any rights if their actions are caused by, or arise from, appraisal or examination allowed under the policy.

- Lines 56 – 67 deals with policy cancellation. It provides that the insured may cancel the policy at any time, and deals with the return of a portion of the paid premium. This section goes on to state that the carrier may also cancel the policy at any time and similarly indicates provisions for possible return of premium. (It should be noted that the latter part of this section, dealing with the company's ability to cancel, would not presently be enforceable in most states within the United States. Generally speaking, there are only limited reasons such as failure of the insured to pay the premium, fraud, etc., that allow the carrier to cancel the policy after issuance.)

- Lines 68 – 85 outlines the rights and obligations of, and to, mortgagees related to the insured property. Again, the company's right to cancel the policy relating to the mortgagee would be severely restricted from what is stated in the policy form by more recent near-universal court decisions and legislative directives that limit cancellation rights. This section also shifts the responsibility from the insured to the mortgagee, in the event the insured fails to do so, for such things as the filing of a Proof of Loss.

- Lines 86 – 89 further defines the loss payment responsibility in the event that other insurance applies. (See lines 25 and 26 of the policy, discussed earlier in this chapter). This later section indicates that if other insurance does exist the liability for the loss will be pro-rated among the covering companies. (See the discussion of "Other Insurance" in Chapter 4, the Basic Policy Format.)

- Lines 90 – 122 sets forth the insured's requirements in case a loss occurs. The insured must give immediate notice to the company, protect the property from further damage, separate damaged and undamaged property and prepare an inventory, and furnish a Proof of Loss form within the prescribed time frame. The section outlines what is to be contained in the Proof of Loss.

- Lines 123 – 140 details the appraisal rights and obligation of both the insured and the carrier in the event the amount of the actual cash value of the property involved, and/or the extent of the damage to the property, cannot be agreed upon. Both the insured and the insurer will select their own appraiser, and the two appraisers will agree on a disinterested umpire. Each appraiser will investigate the loss and submit to the other their assessment as to value and damage. Any disagreed upon figures will then be submitted to the umpire who will issue his findings as to the figures with which he agrees. This will be the loss value. (See Chapter 5, Legal Issues).

- Lines 141 – 147 gives the company the options to take any or all of the damaged property at the agreed or apprised value, and/or to repair, rebuild or replace the property "... with other of like kind and quality within a reasonable time ...." (See the first page of this chapter dealing with the ACV loss adjustment basis.)

- Lines 148 – 149 prohibits the insured from abandoning any property to the insurance company.

- Lines 150 – 156 directs the company to pay for the agreed upon damages within 60 days of receipt of the Proof of Loss filed by the insured.

- Lines 157 – 161 indicates suit against the company by the insured can only be commenced if all the requirements in the policy have been complied with, and if the suit is commenced within 12 months following the inception of the policy. (Note that in most jurisdictions the 12 month restriction would be contrary to the statute of limitations in the applicable jurisdiction in which the suit would be brought. Generally the statute of limitations would not begin until the loss occurs, rather than the policy issuance date unless the issue in dispute was one of contractual propriety, etc.) (See Chapter, 5, Legal Issues, the section entitled Legal Action/Civil Litigation.)

- Lines 162 – 165 deals with Subrogation and requires the insured to assign to the carrier any or all of the insured's rights of recovery against any party, to the extent the company has made a loss payment under the policy.

As with all other policy forms, it is necessary to read the entire policy for the type of coverage being reviewed.

CHAPTER TEN

The Commercial General Liability Insurance Policy

T he Commercial General Liability Insurance Policy is designed to provide protection for commercial entities against claims and suit brought against them, and arising out of their actions, the actions of their employees or others for whom they are responsible, or from the products or services that they provide.

As with all other types of policies, the Declarations Page will set forth the name of the insured, the primary location, the premium, and the individual coverages that will be provided, with the corresponding limits of liability.

The Insuring Agreement will set forth the coverages and define these areas to provide the parameters of the protection being afforded. Most General Liability policies will provide both defense and indemnification. The Insuring clause will usually state something such as:

*"We (the insurer) will pay those sums that the insured
becomes legally obligated to pay as damages because
of bodily injury, property damage, personal injury, or
advertising injury to which this insurance applies. We will
have the right and duty to defend any lawsuit seeking those
damages. We may, at our discretion, investigate any occurrence and settle any claim or lawsuit that may result."*

The policy will go on to define many of the specific terms contained in the identifying paragraphs such as the one quoted above.

In addition to the obligation to pay for such damages as are outlined, and those that specifically relate to the insured's legal obligation to someone else, the policy will most often provide certain
other "supplemental' payments. These additional payments are
usually associated with the handling of the claims and suits that
the insurer will be undertaking. For example, the insurer will pay
for the expenses they incur in the handling of the matter at hand,
including legal fees and expenses incurred in defending the insured.
They will agree to pay for bail bonds if such charges are necessary
and related to the incident giving rise to the claim or suit. If the
insured incurs any costs at the request of the insurer, those costs
will be reimbursed. If there are interest charges assessed on any
legal judgment, the carrier will pay those. Some policies may have
other supplemental payment provisions, and each policy in question must be read to fully determine what is to be paid.

It should be noted that although the Declarations Page may indicate the primary or sole location of the insured's business, the CGL
policy coverages are not confined to only those incidents occurring
at or near those premises. The CGL policy is based on the insured's
activities, products, services, etc., regardless of where the incident
occurs, (subject to wording in the policy itself that may post certain
geographical restrictions, such as only covering activities in the

United States, or in North American, etc.)

Another type of protection generally provided is for Medical Payments. This will pay for medical expenses incurred by anyone who is injured by the insured, by their employees or agents, their products or services, the condition of the premises. etc. In other words, the same people who might bring a claim or suit against the insured under the Liability portion of the policy can register a claim for their medical damages under the Medical Payments coverage. The difference between these two coverages, as far as the medical costs reimbursement is concerned, is that under the Liability portion of the policy, the insured must be legally responsible for the medical costs. (See Tort Liability in Chapter 5, Legal Issues.) Under the Medical Payments coverage, the reimbursement is made without regard to fault or legal liability.

As with the Liability section of the policy, the benefits under the Medical Payments section are not limited to incidents that occur at or near the insured's premises. The policy is intended to provide protection for the insured's activities, products, etc., and since those activities or products may be at locations other than the insured's premises, the coverages are not location specific.

Usually contained within the Insuring Agreement section of the policy (although they may sometimes be found in other areas), are some pertinent definitions. These are provided to assist the insured and the carrier in identifying certain qualifying individuals, actions, and situations. In this area there is usually a definition of who is insured under the policy. There may be slight variations depending on whether the insured entity is an individual, a partnership, a joint venture, a corporation, etc. Once again, the policy must be read to determine who qualifies as an insured, but often it will include employees, officers of the insured company, some vendors, members of newly acquired organizations, and volunteers.

Within the CGL policy there are numerous Exclusions that limit and better define the coverages contained in the Insuring Agreement section.

Under the Liability section, some exclusions often seen are those that indicate the coverage does not apply to injury or damage that:

- is expected or intended by the insured;

- arises from the assuming of liability under a contract (although this can often be purchased as a separate coverage);

- arises from the serving or distributing of alcoholic beverages;

- occurs to an employee if the injury arises in the course and scope of their employment;

- involves any other obligations under workers' compensation laws;

- arises from the release, etc., of pollutants;

- arises from the ownership, maintenance or use of an automobile, watercraft or aircraft;

- arises from professional services being provided by the insured;

- occurs to property owned, rented to, or occupied by the insured;

- arises due to war, whether declared or not;

- occurs to the insured's work or work product; and

- involves loss of use of property if that property has not been physically damaged or destroyed.

Note that many of the exclusions relating to injury and damage can be insured against under other separate policies better suited for such incidents.

There are also exclusions relating to Medical Payments coverage, and some that relate to both Liability and Medical Payments. Under Medical Payments, expenses incurred for injury to an insured are not covered. Note the differences here between Medical Payments under the CGL policy and Medical Payments in the Automobile policy. (See Chapter 7.) Also not covered in the Medical Payments section of the CGL are expenses incurred for an injury to an employee of the insured (whether covered by Workers' Compensation insurance or not); injuries to tenants residing and/or renting any portion of the insured premises; injuries incurred during athletic activities; and injuries arising from declared or undeclared war.

Most General Liability insurance policies contain a broad exclusion for all coverages relating to nuclear energy, or the use of other hazardous properties.

In the Conditions section the carrier will set forth such things as the insured's duties in the event of an occurrence, claim or suit; what legal action can or cannot be taken against the company by the insured if a dispute between the two arises; failure to disclose certain hazards; and "Other Insurance". (For more information on the Other Insurance Clause, see Chapter 4, "The Basic Insurance Policy Format.")

In addition to those definitions sometimes found in the Insuring Agreement, there may be other terms and conditions defined or discussed in the Conditions section.

Beyond the basic tenets of the Commercial General Liability Policy, some entities need to expand, elaborate, or otherwise mold the policy to fit their specific needs. For example, a gas station, parking lot or auto repair facility may need to add a section for Garage Keepers Legal Liability. (See Chapter 15.) This will change certain precepts of the CGL to conform to the needs of a company engaged in such activities. As indicated earlier, there is an exclusion under the Liability section for damage to property in the care, custody or control of the insured. These entities (gas stations, parking lots, auto repair facilities, etc.) need coverage to protect them against claims by the owners of those vehicles the insured has taken into their "care, custody, or control." This need also exists for companies taking possession of items other than automobiles, such as tailors or dry cleaners, and a similar endorsement of the policy would be necessary for them as well.

An establishment in the business of serving alcoholic beverages may need an endorsement to provide for Liquor Liability (excluded under the basic CGL form); a professional (such as an architect or accountant), may need to include Professional Liability Coverage (also generally excluded under the CGL contract).

In considering the aspects of the CGL policy, it is necessary to read the specific form at issue in order to determine exactly what coverages are provided, the exclusions that apply, and the definitions of the various terms used in the policy language.

CHAPTER ELEVEN

The Commercial Multi-Peril (Package) Insurance Policy

In the middle of the 20th century, the insurance industry developed a new type of policy form – or more accurately, a form that combined existing coverages into a single policy aimed specifically at business concerns. This new form was the Commercial Multi-Peril policy, also known as the "package" policy.

Businesses were already protected with fire policies, general liability coverages, policies protecting them from theft, burglary, etc. Each of these was, however, a separate form, often written through different brokers, and with different carriers. The package policy was an attempt to consolidate the coverages into a single form for easier usage and, often, at a reduced premium.

FIRST PARTY COVERAGES:

The coverages contained in the primary property sections of the policy usually extended to (but were not necessarily limited to) such things as damage to buildings (owned or rented), business property, money & securities, accounts receivables, valuable papers, employee dishonesty, computers and intellectual property, forgery, counterfeit papers, etc.

The perils insured against in this section of the package policy generally duplicate those found in the commercial fire policy and the business property policy, but are usually somewhat broader. The underwriter is often more comfortable with the carrier's ability to control many of the losses since the presence of other carriers and policy forms can be avoided. This leads to expanded coverage protection, often at a reduced premium.

As with most other "first party' coverages, the package policy similarly excludes aircraft, automobiles and other motor vehicles, watercraft, land, trees and shrubs, etc. There are specific limitations as to the amount collectable for furs, jewelry, gems, precious metals, etc.

An included coverage is for the loss of business income if the business' operations are required to be suspended due to a specific loss that is covered under the policy.

Many of the exclusions under this property section of the policy are those found in other property policies. The coverage does not apply to such things as earth movement, nuclear hazards, war, flood, mudslides, etc.

One or more deductibles may apply to the various coverages included in this section of the policy. The deductibles may differ as to the various coverages being provided. Since the forms offered by various carriers may differ, it is necessary to review the language in a specific policy if a more detailed analysis is needed.

THIRD PARTY COVERAGES:

The second primary section of the package policy is the Business Liability section, and is quite similar to the Commercial General Liability policy (see Chapter 10). This section may also incorporate other commercial liability coverages such as those found in the Commercial Automobile policy (including hired and non-owned automobile coverage), and/or certain "miscellaneous" coverages (see Chapter 15) such as the Garage Keeper's Policy, the Condominium Association policy, etc.

The general protections provided include basic liability protection for bodily injury, property damage, personal injury and advertising liability. Medical expense coverage is generally included, as well as some limited professional services coverage.

Since the policy is written to protect a business entity, those insured under the policy would include the named insured designated in the declarations, employees, the spouse of a sole proprietor, all partners of a partnership, and, for other types of organizations, the executive officers. The coverage would extend to newly acquired businesses, and to volunteers under certain defined circumstances. In addition to these specific insureds, the policy also extends coverage to others under certain precise situations. (The policy form should be reviewed for the specifics of such added insured identification.)

Most package policies also contain a Broad Form Vendors Endorsement. In the event the business entity being insured agrees to provide coverage to a vendor, that vendor would be covered for bodily injury and property damages under this section of the policy. This endorsement only applies to such injury or damage arising out of the goods and/or services provided by the named insured. As with most Vendor's Endorsements, the coverage here is not intended to protect the vendor from their own actions that may be independent of those associated with the named insured's products and services.

Exclusions under this section of the policy run similar to those in the Commercial General Liability policy (see Chapter 10).

Many of the policy conditions are also similar to those found in other commercial policies and relate to cancellation, misrepresentation, inspection of records by the carrier, the Other Insurance Clause (which may differ between the property section and the liability section), and the duties of the insured in the event of a loss or claim.

As has been pointed out elsewhere in this book, it is important to review the specific policy in question if there are questions about the content or provisions of a particular insurance contract.

CHAPTER TWELVE

The Workers' Compensation Policy

As was discussed in Chapter 1, "A Brief History of Insurance", Workers' Compensation insurance came about as a plan to try to equalize the relative positions of strength between employees injured while working, and their employers. The advantages had been generally stacked in favor of the employers, and the legislative enactments to provide benefits enabled the injured employee to survive economically after his injury, and to receive prompt and adequate medical attention when needed.

A *quid pro quo* for the employer providing these benefits was that the employees lost some of their rights to sue an employer for negligence, and possibly obtain large sums of money for their injuries through the civil courts. Workers' Compensation benefits, and payments made under this insurance coverage, are not derived from common law (See Chapter 5,Legal Issues), but rather are mandated by specific legislation passed, and applicable, in each individual state. While many of the benefits are similar from state to state, there are understandably various nuances — not only in amounts payable, but also for types of injuries covered, circumstances involving coverage, the dispute resolution process, etc.

Due to the need for insurance carriers to provide requisite coverage forms that are applicable in all states, the standard Workers' Compensation policy is, by design, generic in many ways. Multiple endorsements are available to the agent and underwriter to personalize the standard policy to fit the needs and requirements of individual states and business entities.

As with other policy types, the Workers' Compensation policy will include a Declaration Page with the insured's (employer's) name, primary business location, the policy period, the states in which coverage will be provided, and the premium. Contained within the policy will also be the Insuring Agreement, Exclusions, and Conditions; however, these areas are not always clearly delineated nor readily identified.

The Workers' Compensation policy has two primary coverages: Coverage A, which is the basic Workers' Compensation coverage protecting the employer and providing benefits for the injured worker(s); and Coverage B, the Employer's Liability Insurance, not to be confused with the Commercial General Liability policy discussed in Chapter 10.

Under Coverage A, the basic Workers' Compensation coverage providing the statutory benefits, there will be no Limit of Liability shown on the Declarations Page. The amounts payable under the various laws to which this coverage applies are mandated by the statutes governing the benefits, including maximum amounts where applicable. The Declarations page will show Limits of Liability for Coverage B, the Employer's Liability coverage, since it is not part of the legislated, mandatory coverage, but rather is provided to address certain very specific risks to the employer arising from injured employee scenarios. This will be discussed in greater detail later in this chapter.

POLICY PREMIUM

Premiums for Workers' Compensation policies are driven by actuarially derived predictions of future losses. While all insurance premiums have some degree of such predictions, the nature of WC coverage is such that it makes the actuary a very important and integral part of the premium determination equation, especially as it pertains to Coverage A. With no Limit of Liability, and with benefits varying from state to state, the anticipation of types of losses and their economic impact can only be speculated upon. The use of actuarial models and trending charts are invaluable in attempting to determine accurate pricing.

The actual premiums are derived in several ways. Perhaps the most prevalent means is by class rating; i.e., employers rated based on the type of business in which they are engaged, and the general rates for such businesses. Because this can be determined for large groups of similar employers, it often provides a solid platform on which to base projections of future losses for any given member of the class.

For larger employers, the rates may be based on the amount of their payroll. This indicator is often used in conjunction with class rating to further distinguish exposure based on size of the insured, as well as the type of employee work activities.

Where payroll is a determining factor in the premium calculations, there will often be an annual audit of the employer's payroll to confirm the amounts of that payroll, as well as the pre-determined classifications for the various jobs within the employer's business.

Certain job types are more dangerous, and therefore produce a higher loss frequency and/or severity. These will tend to increase premium levels.

The premiums on many policies are adjusted periodically (usually annually) based on the loss experience of the employer; i.e., how many accidents occurred, what was the payment total, etc. With an employer having relatively low loss frequency and severity, the premium might be reduced. On the opposite end of the spectrum, an employer suffering more losses than were anticipated might be surcharged for additional premium. This modification of premium based on the exposure to the insurer, is referred to as the Exposure Modifier or the "X-Mod."

In some instances, with an insured of sufficient size, and one with a long loss history, a special actuarial study might be conducted to predict future loss history and thereby predict the future loss exposure to the insurer. Such an actuarial study would then be an integral part of determining the premium rate for that employer.

COVERAGE A: Workers Compensation Insurance

It is within this coverage that the primary benefits are found. As indicated previously, the policy is purposely written generically so as to broadly cover the employer's responsibility to their workers. The insuring clause may simply state "Coverage A of this policy applies to the Workers' Compensation laws of the states listed in this Declarations Page."

Since monetary benefits, eligibility requirements, medical treatment restrictions, etc., may all vary from one state to another, and since Coverage A provides coverage wherever benefits are allowed and applicable, it is important that the Workers' Compensation policy address the specifics of the state(s) involved.

If an employer conducts operations in more than one state, it is imperative that the policy be properly endorsed to include the necessary amendments to address the requirements incorporated in the various state W.C. laws and codes.

It is also possible that the employer, at the time the policy is issued, will not have any known or suspected activities in other states. Nevertheless, the possibility remains that one or more employees might be assigned, either temporarily or permanently, to work in another state. It is also possible that the employer may hire someone in one state and have that individual work in a different state. That can be a determining and pivotal issue in some situations. Most insurers provide an "All States Endorsement" which extends the applicable coverage to respond to an accident occurring in any of the United States, even if the employer has no facility in, or did not anticipate activities in, that state.

The inclusion of multiple endorsements for various states, and/or the use of an "All States" endorsement, may impact the premium charges. Activities in multiple states could pose a greater risk for higher payments than might be seen from coverage for a single state in which the employer is operating.

The location (state) where the injury occurs is important, but there are some instances when the place of accident is not the governing fact. Some jurisdictions determine which state's benefits will apply based on where the injured worker was hired, rather than where the injury occurred. Therefore, if a person is injured in State A, but had been hired in State B, and if both states adhere to the "point of hire" doctrine, then the Workers' Compensation benefits for State B would apply. If both states were "place of accident" states, then obviously the jurisdiction in which the accident occurred would be the applicable jurisdiction. If only one of the states was a "point of hire" state, and the other was a "place of accident" state, generally the injured worker may choose the jurisdiction most favorable to his situation.

Under Workers' Compensation coverage, not all injuries, illnesses, sicknesses, etc., are deemed to be "compensable", or allowed, under the coverage. In order for an injury, illness, or sickness to be deemed to be compensable it must "arise out of the course and scope of the employment." That is to say, the problem must come about from an activity directly and naturally resulting from the employee's work duties and responsibilities; i.e., "arising from the course of the work. " It must also be "in the scope of the employment"; i.e., referring to the time, place and circumstances of the incident as relating to nature, conditions, obligations and incidents of the employment.

When a compensable accident occurs, the employer is usually required to prepare and file with the State a "First Report of Accident" form. This sets out the basic facts of the accident, injury, etc., and is the first step toward the injured worker qualifying for the benefits due under that state's Workers' Compensation laws.

Once an injured worker (or his employer on the worker's behalf) files a claim for Workers' Compensation benefits, the insurance company providing the coverage will undertake an investigation of the facts surrounding the incident. This may include contact with the injured worker, with management employees, co-workers, witnesses, third party participants, the treating physician or clinic, and anyone else who might have information about the matter.

Benefits:

In most jurisdictions the basic Workers' Compensation benefits are similar. There could be, however, some major and important differences that need to be recognized and understood. Rates of payment to injured workers may differ; there may be specific waiting periods before benefits begin; the requirements for medical treatment may differ; methodology to determine disability and resultant settlement values may vary; and other specific differences may also exist. Under Coverage A, a worker sustaining an injury in the course and scope of his employment would be entitled to seek benefits as set forth in the Workers' Compensation laws of the applicable state.

Medical Treatment:

If the employee is in need of medical treatment, the insurance company will authorize treatment for the injured worker with a physician or clinic familiar with the Workers' Compensation laws and benefits. Some jurisdictions allow workers to immediately select their own medical provider, and some allow such personal physician utilization only after a certain post-injury period of time.

Since an integral part of Workers' Compensation benefits in all jurisdictions is the providing of immediate and competent medical attention to treat the injury, a qualified injured worker is entitled to be seen by a physician, to be hospitalized if necessary, to receive prescribed drugs and pharmaceuticals, to receive authorized and prescribed physical therapy, and possibly psychological counseling if medically justified.

Some states mandate the injured worker be treated by a physician of the employer's choice. In certain jurisdictions, this employer designated physician involvement is only applicable for a specific limited period of time, after which the injured worker is free to see a physician or other caregiver of his choice. In other jurisdictions, the injured employee is free to seek treatment from the medical facility of their choice with no control by the employer.

Temporary Total Disability/Temporary Partial Disability:

If, for a limited period of time following a compensable accident, a worker were unable to continue working, he or she would be entitled to periodic (usually weekly or bi-weekly) maintenance payments. These benefits are known as "Temporary Total Disability" (TTD) payments (although some jurisdictions may have a slightly different terminology.)

The amount of these TTD payments (and in some cases the duration of the payments) is governed by the Workers' Compensation laws for the state having jurisdiction. The calculation of the TTD payments may be based on a percentage of the employee's average wages, on the marital status of the employee, the number of dependants, or any other number of variables set forth in the laws of the state that governs the injury. There is generally a minimum and maximum weekly amount allowed for these TTD payments.

TTD continues as long as the treating physician (or a specialist to whom the injured worker has been referred for assessment) indicates the employee is unable to return to his normal occupation. In some instances, the employer may provide other, temporary employment for the injured worker which is less strenuous than his normal occupation, but within the confines of his medical restrictions. This would allow the employee to return to work (albeit in a different capacity) and TTD benefits would cease or be reduced. If the employee returns to this temporary alternative employment, but does not receive his same previous wage, he would be entitled to Temporary Partial Disability payments. Again, while this will differ between states and jurisdictions, the concept of such TPD payments is to supplement the earnings for the injured worker.

Permanent Partial Disability:

When, in the opinion of the treating physician, the injured worker has reached maximum medical recovery, their condition is said to be "permanent and stationary". At this point, TTD will generally be halted, even if the employee has not yet been able to return to work. When the maximum medical recovery is attained, the injured worker will be assessed as to whether or not there is any perma-nent residual disability from the injury. If so, the employee may be entitled to an award for Permanent Partial Disability (PPD).

The process for assessing the degree of PPD, and the monetary compensation related to that specific degree of disability, varies widely from state to state. Generally there must be a medical "rating" by the treating physician, or a doctor to whom the worker has been referred for such an assessment, or a specially trained individual whose job it is to convert the medical information into a disability rating.

Once the amount and/or degree of PPD is established, then the monetary value of that disability is calculated and may vary depending on any number of facts or circumstances related to the injured worker. In order to become better versed on this aspect, it is necessary for the reader to become familiar with the specifics of the Workers' Compensation laws in the applicable jurisdiction.

In most jurisdictions, the philosophy behind PPD is that the injured worker, with permanent disability, will suffer some degree of reduced future wage loss. The PPD monetary settlement is designed to alleviate or minimize that loss of earning power. In reality, PPD settlements are often made even though there is no demonstrable evidence of any future wage loss resulting from the injury. Such payments are usually made for expedience, in order to finalize and close the WC claim.

In some jurisdictions, the amount of PPD is paid to the worker in weekly, bi-weekly or monthly installments until the total amount of the award is satisfied. Other jurisdictions allow for the PPD award to be paid in a single lump sum amount.

Apportionment of Permanent Disability:

In many states, the net total amount of allowable permanent dis-ability is limited, depending on how many previous injuries or accidents have been suffered by a single individual. In certain states, disability may be awarded as a percentage of disability to the body as a whole, or to a specific part of the body; i.e., 22% of the left arm, or 14% of the right leg, etc.

Under those circumstances, if the employee suffers a subsequent injury to the same body part, there would be a "set-off" to take "credit" for the prior disability award. For instances, if a first accident resulted in a PPD award of 16% of the right arm, and a second injury to the same body part resulted in a revised PPD rating of 27%, the injured worker would only be entitled to an award of 11% PPD for the second injury - - the amount of the current disability, less the amount from the previous injury. Theoretically, the total amount that can ever be received would be 100% of the body as a whole, or any given body part. This process of revising the amount of the PPD award based on credit from prior injuries is referred to as "apportionment."

Permanent Total Disability:

In addition to the benefits for TTD and PPD, basically all states also provide for disability that is permanent, but not partial; i.e., total disability. This is referred to as Permanent Total Disability (PTD) and indicates the injured employee will be unable to return to any gainful employment as a result of the disability sustained from the compensable injury. In effect, this is a lifetime pension.

As with TTD and PPD, it is necessary to have medical evidence that the employee is disabled to the extent that would qualify him for this benefit. Again, the specific amounts and other nuances of this lifetime pension can only be determined by studying the specific aspects of the Workers' Compensation laws in the applicable jurisdiction.

Second Injury Funds:

Several states have enacted legislation whereby the compensation payable to an injured worker for an injury will, in effect, not be "apportioned" (see above), due to a previous injury to the same body. This is accomplished, in most jurisdictions, through the establishment of a Second Injury Fund.

The compensation award under such a scenario would normally be reduced due to the apportionment discussed above. In states with a Second Injury Fund, the Workers' Compensation insurer would still only be liable for the apportioned amount, and the Fund would pay the balance of the award. The employer would not be charged with this added payment.

These Second Injury Funds are usually financed by a small tax assessed on all W.C. premiums written in the state, and are usually administered by an appropriate state agency or facility.

Vocational Rehabilitation:

Some jurisdictions contain opportunities for the injured employee who has been rated as PTD or PPD to receive vocational rehabilitation. This provides training so the injured worker can return to work in some profession or employment field different from that in which he was engaged at the time of the injury. During this vocational training, the employee is usually paid a maintenance allowance (much like the TTD payments) until the training has been completed and the person has been reintroduced into the work force. Since the person, once trained, would be able to be employed with reduced, if any, restrictions, the PTD monetary award might be lost, or the PPD award might be reduced, depending on the specifics of the state laws that govern.

Death Benefits:

Since some work place injuries result in death of the employee, almost all Workers' Compensation laws provide for death benefits to be paid to the deceased's beneficiaries. As with other benefits under these laws, each state will vary as to the amount of such death benefits and how they are calculated.

Dispute Resolution:

In the event the employer (and/or the insurer) dispute the compensability (applicability) of the accident, the injury, the permanent nature of the injury, etc., then all or a part of the claim for benefits may be denied. In that case, the injured worker has certain rights under the Workers' Compensation laws to contest the denial of benefits.

Those rights and avenues of contestability vary widely from jurisdiction to jurisdiction. In all states there is some legal forum (referees, commissioners, panels, judges, etc.) to which the injured worker may take his or her case to attempt to obtain Workers' Compensation benefits, or to reinstate denied benefits.

The contestability avenues are usually also available if there are disputed issues related to the injury itself, the amount or duration of TTD, the existence and/or degree of PPD, etc.

Generally speaking, the Workers' Compensation dispute forums are much less formal than the civil court proceedings. The scope, direction, and parameters of the hearings are shaped by the local laws, years of tradition, and accepted procedures within the system.

United States Federal Benefits:

As noted, each state has Workers' Compensation legislation that contains similar, although not necessarily identical, wording to provide benefits for employees injured while in the course and scope of their employment. There is another similar set of laws that may, under certain circumstances, involve injured employees in a given state.

This is the Longshoremen's and Harbor Workers' Compensation Act. An employee who is injured while loading or unloading a sea-going vessel may be covered under the Workers' Compensation laws for the state in which the accident occurs (or as mentioned earlier, under the laws of the state of hire). If the accident occurs on the dockside, or on land, this would be the case.

If, however, the injury occurs while the worker is onboard the vessel (in navigable waters, which includes vessels moored at dock, piers, etc.), the injury would be covered under the Federal Harbor Workers' and Longshoremen's Act. Claims under this set of Federal laws are administered by the United States Department of Labor. Although the Federal Act is not specifically discussed here, it is recommended that a copy of the Act be reviewed in the event it appears that an incident would be covered by these laws involving a vessel being loaded or unloaded.

COVERAGE B: Employer's Liability Insurance

As can be seen from a review of many of the coverages affording civil liability protection to employers, most exclude such protection for injuries or damages to their employees. (See General Liability Policy, Chapter 10; Mullti-Peril Policy, Chapter 11; and Excess Liability Policy, Chapter 13). Nevertheless, there are certain limited situations that can arise which result in employers having a civil liability exposure to an employee, (even those injured while in the course and scope of their employment). Therefore, in order to provide coverage in such situations, the Workers' Compensation Policy includes, as Coverage B, Employer's Liability Coverage.

This added protection is a standard part of almost every Workers'

Compensation policy provided in virtually every state. The claims under this coverage are relatively few.

One example of a situation where the coverage would come into play involves an injured worker bringing claim and/or suit against a third party. The third party counter-sues or cross- complains against the injured worker's employer, alleging the employer to be negligent.

Although such allegations would usually be covered by the employer's General Liability insurance policy, that policy would have an exclusion for injury to an employee. Therefore, the Workers' Compensation policy, under Coverage B, would cover the employer for this civil liability exposure.

This is merely one scenario that would bring Coverage B into play. There are other similar situations where the coverage might also become activated.

CHAPTER THIRTEEN

The Excess Liability (Umbrella) Policy

Very often the limits of liability provided in one or more underlying liability policies may be insufficient to cover the damages an insured incurs, or to which it is exposed. Therefore, there exists the opportunity to purchase additional coverage that is "layered" above the coverage provided in these underlying policies. This additional coverage is known as excess insurance. Since they may also cover a number of separate underlying policies written for an insured, they are at times referred to as umbrella policies, providing protection over a group of policies.

Excess coverage may be written on a personal or commercial basis. A personal excess policy would be written to protect an individual or family, and might provide coverage over the liability sections in a Homeowner's policy, and/or the Personal Automobile policy. Commercial Excess policies might provide added protection above a General Liability policy, a Commercial Automobile policy, a Workers' Compensation policy, Errors and Omissions, Professional Liability, Directors' and Officers' coverage, or any other basic liability policy written for a business or governmental entity.

In some instances, there will be more than one excess policy written, with each policy providing coverage above a certain level so that multiple excess policies will be layered — one on top of the other — to provide ever increasing levels of coverage.

In most instances the excess coverage is written as a "following form" contract. That is to say, although the excess policies themselves will have certain terms and conditions, exclusions, etc., they will basically conform to the coverage provided in the underlying policy that they are protecting.

A substantial difference between the primary coverages and the excess form is that in excess policies there is generally no requirement to provide a defense for the policyholder in the event of a lawsuit being filed against any insured. This defense obligation is most often the responsibility of the underlying, primary policy.

The excess policy may come into effect for some defense responsibility in the event the limits of the underlying policy have been exhausted (assuming this relieves the underlying carrier from further defense obligations), or in that rare situation where the underlying policy may be able to withdraw from defense due to exclusionary wording, inception/expiration anomalies, etc. This is referred to as a "drop down" on the part of the excess carrier.

Another difference between primary coverage and excess protection is that the reporting requirements under an excess form may be different than those found in a primary policy. Some excess policies require that a claim be incurred and also reported to the carrier within the policy term; i.e., between inception and expiration (although an extended reporting time frame may be purchased for this reporting requirement.)

Since excess coverage, as noted above, may be purchased in "layers", there may be several excess policies written to protect an insured entity. As the coverages are layered upward, the unit cost continues to decline. Therefore an entity with substantial risk might purchase a primary liability policy with a $1 million limit of liability, then purchase a "first layer excess" policy for an additional $5 million of coverage. That may be "topped" with a $20 million excess policy, which might have another $50 million above that, and so forth. In the above example, the first layer excess would be said to be "$5 million, x-of $1 million." The next layer would be said to be "$20 million, x-of $6 million. " The third layer would be "$50 million x-of $26 million." In this example the insured would have a total of $76 million in coverage if needed.

The cost per $1,000 of coverage for the primary policy would be greater than the unit price for the first layer excess. Not only would the defense costs be factored into the underlying policy pricing, it is anticipated that loss frequency would be substantially greater than it would be for the higher threshold excess policies. The first layer excess unit cost would then be higher than the next layer since it would "come into play" before the higher levels, and so forth up to the highest level of excess coverage purchased.

As is the case in determining other specific coverages, including terms and conditions, the reader considering the aspects of a particular excess policy is urged to review the specific excess policy form itself, along with any and all underlying policies that may be at issue.

Chapter Fourteen

The Reinsurance Policy

As noted in the earlier sections of this text, in addition to policies of insurance written on a primary and/or excess basis, there are also policies that reinsure other carriers for exposures they undertake. This is done through the issuance of reinsurance policies.

Insurance companies enter into reinsurance relationships through Reinsurance Treaties or through Facultative Agreements. These are called "placements."

A Reinsurance Treaty will set out an agreement between the writer of the underlying insurance (the cedant) and one or more reinsurance companies, indicating that the ceding company agrees to submit, and the reinsurer agrees to accept, all business in a certain class, line of business, location, type, etc. The reinsurance becomes, in effect, automatic so long as the risk fits within the parameters of the treaty wording.

Facultative Reinsurance is accomplished by the writer of the underlying insurance (the cedant) approaching a reinsurer with a particular piece of business, to attempt to reach an agreement as to the amount and type of reinsurance that will be offered and accepted. It is done on a risk-by-risk basis.

Within the insurance industry, the functions of reinsurance are understood to be (1) increasing capacity for the ceding company, (2) protecting the ceding company from catastrophe losses, (3) stabilizing the ceding company's underwriting results by minimizing wild fluctuations in underwriting ratios, (4) improving policy holder surplus for the ceding company, and (5) lending the reinsurer's technical skills to those of the ceding company.

Reinsurance can be written as Proportional (Pro Rata) coverage, or as Non-Proportional/Excess of Loss coverage. Proportional reinsurance is either Quota Share or Surplus Share. Non-Proportional reinsurance is written as either Per Risk /Per Occurrence Excess of Loss, or as Per Aggregate Excess of Loss.

Quota Share reinsurance is written to share any loss "from the ground up", as opposed to only coming into effect after a loss reaches a certain level. The respective percentages of the loss to be paid by the ceding carrier and by the reinsurer are set in the reinsurance contract between the parties.

Surplus Share also involves a sharing of all losses; however, the percentage shared by the reinsurer will vary for different risks covered by the agreement.

In Non-Proportional, Per Risk/Per Occurrence Excess of Loss, the reinsurance involvement may come into play whenever the loss exceeds a certain amount that is originally specified in the reinsurance agreement. If it is written on a Per Risk basis, then the reinsurer would be responsible for losses over the pre-agreed retention amount for <u>any specific insured</u> and for a specific loss. On a Per Occurrence basis, the reinsurer would be responsible for losses exceeding the retained limit for all losses incurred and arising from a single occurrence <u>regardless of how many insured risks</u> might have incurred a loss from the same incident or occurrence. (This is often critical in situations arising from natural disasters such as floods, hurricanes, etc. In such instances, the basis of the reinsurance — Per Risk or Per Occurrence — is extremely important.)

In Non-Proportional, Per Aggregate Excess of Loss reinsurance, the reinsurer participates over a predetermined aggregate limit of loss for a number of risks over a specific period of time.

The agreement between the cedant and the reinsurer is governed by the same duties and responsibilities as are found in all other contracts and agreements, such as "good faith", etc; however, in this case there is yet another, very important, duty. The reinsurer is said to "follow the fortunes" of the cedant. The reinsurance contract may have certain specific conditions and exclusions that would dictate much of what transpires between the parties. Nevertheless, the reinsurer is bound to pay their portion of losses for which the ceding company is responsible, unless the type of loss is specifically excluded from the reinsurance contract. The reinsurer may have corporate rules or admonitions on certain loss handling and payments, etc., but they could not be enforced if the cedant had no such rules, and legitimately went forward with accepting the loss. The reinsurer must follow the fortunes of the ceding company.

At times, an unlicensed or non-admitted primary insurance carrier (See Chapter 2) will obtain a piece of primary or excess insurance business by having a licensed insurer write the business, and then reinsure 100% of the account with the unlicensed or nonadmitted carrier. This is called Fronting, with the licensed carrier being the "front" for the unlicensed carrier. While this practice may, on its face, sound questionable or even fraudulent, most such arrangements are legitimate, legal, and accepted by the various State Insurance Departments. They often provide a genuine need for an insured, and can provide insurance coverage for specific areas, types of risk, or risks needing large and stable insurance protection.

Many of the same concerns or desires that drive insurance carriers (cedants) to seek and obtain reinsurance, also apply to the reinsurers (assuming companies) themselves. That is, the reasons specified above for an insurer entering into a reinsurance agreement might also apply to the reinsurer itself. Therefore, reinsurers may reinsure their own reinsurance writings. These agreements are know as Retrocessions. Here the reinsurer, seeking the reinsurance for their own writings, is call the Retrocedant, and the company accepting the reinsurance from the retrocedant is called the Retrocessionaire.

CHAPTER FIFTEEN

Miscellaneous Policies

ERRORS AND OMISSIONS LIABILITY POLICY:

Almost every enterprise is in need of some type of protection against claims and/or lawsuits that might arise from the general conduct of their business. Errors and Omissions coverage does not protect against such things as bodily injury or property damage that may arise from the actions or activities of the insured, their employees, or their products. Those would normally be covered by their Automobile, General Liability, and/or Multi-Peril insurance (See Chapters 7, 10, and 11).

Claims may arise, however, from such things as others relying on the advice, suggestions, or other professional services being rendered by the insured. The above mentioned coverages usually exclude claims arising out of the professional services being offered by the insured. Therefore, the Errors and Omissions policy is needed to provide such coverage under certain specific circumstances.

The Errors and Omissions policy provides that the insurer will pay for damages for which the insured is legally obligated, arising from the insured's wrongful act(s) in rendering or failing to render professional services. As with most other types of coverage, this policy will only respond if the wrongful act is committed during the policy period; however, unlike most other policy types, the wrongful act must also be reported to the insurer during the policy period (or in an "extended reporting period", if the insured purchases this added extension of coverage.)

Another difference between this E&O policy and many other more basic policy forms is that the limit of liability under the E&O form usually includes claims expenses. In other words, as claims expenses are incurred, the remaining applicable and available monetary policy protection is eroded. This is true of many "professional liability" coverages, and is not generally seen in most other basic liability or property policies, (although it may sometimes be included in certain excess policies.)

Many E&O policies (as with other professional liability coverages) contain a "Retention" amount. This acts as a deductible and requires the insured to pay this amount before the insurer becomes liable for any payment of loss or expense. The amount of the retention will be shown on the Declarations Page of the policy in question. Unlike a deductible, the insurer will usually not be involved with the investigation, adjustment or settlement of a loss valued within the retention amount. This also means the insurer will generally not incur or reimburse such expenses as attorney fees, adjuster costs, etc., unless and until the loss reaches or exceeds the retention threshold.

As was the situation discussed above relating to the excess liability policy, the E&O policy also generally requires that the insured not only incur the loss during the policy period, but that the incident giving rise to the claim also be reported to the insurer during that same policy period, (or within the time frame of an extended reporting period, if that is purchased separately.)

In addition to the E&O policy excluding claims arising from bodily injury or property damage, the policy also contains exclusions for claims arising from:

- dishonest, fraudulent, criminal or malicious act, or any knowing violation of the law;

- actual or alleged discharge of pollutants;

- sale or solicitation to sell or to buy securities;

- RICO violation(s);

- breach of a fiduciary duty regarding employee benefits or pension plans;

- employment practices including such things as hiring or termination discrimination, etc.;

- misappropriation of trade secrets or infringement of patent, copyright, trademark, etc.;

- false advertising, antitrust, unfair competition, restraint of trade, etc.;

- contractual or agreement disputes;

- business fees disputes;

- false arrest, libel, slander, defamation, or wrongful eviction.

In any given E&O policy there may be other additional exclusions, and some of the above exclusion examples may not be included or may vary in wording, scope, etc. It is necessary to review the specific policy being considered in any given situation.

The "Other Insurance Clause" in the E&O policy may be Excess, Pro-Rated, or Exculpatory. (See Chapter 4, The Basic Policy Format). There may also be a further extension of this potentially limiting clause to reduce the insurer's responsibility in the event the acts or omissions are of some duration and extend over more than one policy period with the same insurer. Again, the specific policy provision(s) must be reviewed.

Since the basic E&O policy is usually generic in its form and content, it is often necessary for an insured to have the policy amended with endorsements that will tailor the policy to the unique needs and requirements of the insured. These endorsements not only become an integral part of the policy itself, but often are the most specific and informative aspects of an E&O policy.

GARAGEKEEPERS' LIABILITY POLICY:

Businesses involved with automobiles — principally automobile dealerships and automobile repair facilities — have special needs due to the nature of much of their activities. "Garage Operations" can be defined as "... the ownership, maintenance or use of locations for garage business and that portion of the roads or other accesses that adjoin these locations." It is basically all operations necessary to conduct a garage business.

These types of entities regularly have automobiles in their possession that do not belong to them, but whose care is entrusted to them. The General Liability, Multi-Peril and the Commercial Automobile Liability policies normally have an exclusion of coverage for damage to items in the insured's "care, custody and control". Therefore, an automobile left at the insured's location for repairs, service, etc., would not be covered if it were damage while in the insured's possession.

The Garagekeepers' Liability policy is designed to eliminate this coverage exclusion, and provide coverage for the insured in this area of anticipated operations. The policy provides collision and comprehensive coverage (including such things as fire, theft, or vandalism) to automobiles left with the insured for repairs, storage, parking, etc.

Usually the coverage does not extend to any contractual obligations, defective parts, or faulty work. Although it is not uncommon to have a service facility loan a temporary replacement vehicle to a car owner who leaves their car with the insured for service, this policy will generally not provide coverage for that loaned automobile. (Coverage for that auto would usually flow from their insured's "fleet" provisions under the Commercial Automobile Policy. The customer with the loaned vehicle would qualify as a "permissive user" under that commercial policy.)

It is also not unheard of for an auto repair facility to be involved with re-building and/or preparing an automobile for participation in a race or demolition show. Claims arising from such preparation activities by the insured are usually not covered under the Garage-keepers' Liability policy.

Often there are one or more deductibles applicable in this type of policy. There may be one for collision, another for comprehensive, and still another possibly for liability. They may be the same or for differing amounts.

RENTER'S/TENANT'S POLICY:

In Chapter 8, we reviewed the Homeowner's Policy. Not everyone, however, owns a home. Many people reside in various size domiciles that are owned by others, but are rented or leased to them. Most of these are apartments, although certainly the owners of houses and condominiums can, and do, rent or lease to other people.

For those people residing in a rented location, there are special insurance needs, including certain items that would be covered by a homeowner's policy, but do not need to be insured by a tenant. Therefore, there is a policy designed for renters.

The physical property; i.e., the dwelling, fences, garages, etc., are not owned by the tenant and therefore cannot be legally insured by them (except by specific contractual agreement.) They have no ownership interest in these property items. Conversely, the renter's personal property, including furnishings, cannot be covered by the landlord, and must be insured by the personal property owner, the renter.

Similarly, the renter needs to obtain liability coverage in the event there is personal injury and/or property damage caused by the renter's actions. The landlord may have coverage (see below) that will become involved for incidents not caused by the renter, but arising out of the physical premises. Such coverage will generally not provide the necessary protection for the renter.

APARTMENT/CONDOMINIUM OWNER'S POLICY:

Not only does the tenant/resident of a rented or leased location have certain specific needs that cannot be addressed properly and adequately via a homeowner's policy, the owner of the rented or leased premises also has insurance needs that are somewhat distinct due to the nature of the business activities; i.e., the rental arrangements.

The Apartment Policy is somewhat of a hybrid between a Homeowner's Policy and a Commercial Multi-Peril Policy, providing coverage for the property itself, as well as coverage for the business enterprise of the rental activity.

The policy will generally insure the property in question for damage, including damage to garages, storage facilities, swimming pools, fences, appurtenant structures, etc. These coverages may be written on a "named peril" or on an "all risk" basis.

This "property" coverage included in the Apartment/Condominium Policy is not unlike the coverage afforded under a Commercial Property Policy, such as the Standard Fire Policy (See Chapter 9), and/or the Property Section of the Multi-Peril Policy (See Chapter 11).

For owners of a condominium who reside in their own condo premises, their insurance needs would be met by the purchase of a homeowner's policy indicating the premises were legally designated as a condominium.

As noted above, the owner of the real property (the landlord) also needs liability coverage for protection from claims and suits emanating from the physical property. The Apartment/Condominium Policy includes liability coverage, much like the Multi-Peril Policy.

PART III

Appendix

Glossary of Terms and Conditions

Author's Note: In addition to the areas within the text of this manual to which this Index refers, the Glossary also contains many terms and conditions that may be of interest and assistance to the reader.

A

Acceptance of Settlement: In negotiations, to finalize a claim or lawsuit, the plaintiff generally will express willingness to pay certain sums, or to take certain actions, in order to end the matter (the Offer). The defendant will express a willingness to make certain monetary or non-monetary concessions in order to finalize a claim or suit (the Acceptance). See Demand For Settlement. See Offer of Settlement.

Accident: A sudden and unforeseen happening, taking place at a definite time and place. See Occurrence.

ACORD Form: A standardized report format for reporting information, such as a loss or claim, to an insurance company.

"Act of God": A happening that occurs not from the action of anyone against whom blame or fault can be assessed. A natural occurrence.

Actual Cash Value (ACV): The value of an item based on what the item is worth at a particular time, considering concepts such as depreciation, betterment, and usage. See Replacement Cost.

Actuary: A person who scientifically and mathematically determines premiums, and projects future claims and loss reserves based on present levels of value.

Ad damnum (Latin): "To the damages." That portion of a lawsuit or other legal pleadings that addresses the amount of money that the plaintiff or filing party is claiming as damages.

Additional Insured Endorsement: An agreement to expand the coverage being provided by an insurance policy to one or more individuals or companies, in addition to the person or company to whom the policy was issued.

Additur: An increase made by the trial court judge to the amount of an award or verdict rendered by a jury. See Remittitur.

Adhesion Contract: A contract to which one party agreed because it was the only apparent way in which to receive certain goods and/or services from the other party, but in which the agreeing party had little or no means to bargain or negotiate due to the lack of relative strength of position between the parties. See Contract of Adhesion.

Adjudication: The rendering of a judgment or ruling in a legal matter.

Adjuster: A person whose responsibility it is for investigating the facts surrounding a situation that gave rise to an insurance claim, determining the existence or lack of applicable insurance coverage under the policy, calculating the degree of damage and/or injury incurred by the claiming party, collecting and verifying the items of damages being submitted, and attempting to amicably resolve the matter between the parties. See Appraiser.

Ad litem (Latin): "For the suit." An appointment of a party to a legal proceeding to "stand in the shoes" of another; i.e., to act as if the appointed person was, in fact, the party to the proceeding. See Guardian Ad Litem.

Admitted Assets: Assets of an insurance entity that are recognized and accepted by State Departments of Insurance for determining the insurers solvency.

Admitted Insurance Company: One which is licensed by a State Department of Insurance to write business in that state, and is thereby subject to all rules and regulations of that state regarding insurance. See Non-Admitted Company.

Affiant: A person making or giving an affidavit. See Affidavit.

Affidavit: A written declaration, given under oath, with the intent to present evidence of certain facts or happenings in a legal matter. See Affiant.

Affirmative Defense: A defense pleading to a complaint which asserts that if the allegations are true there is a specific defense which would automatically apply.

Agency: The legal relationship which exists between two people or entities when one is acting on behalf of the other (as an Agent), and where the actions, toward a third party, of the person acting as an agent may be imputed back to the person who the agent represents. See Agent. See Bailment. See Master-Servant Doctrine.

Agent: A person acting on behalf of another. Under tort liability, the principle, upon whose benefit the agent is acting, is held accountable for the actions of the agent, including acts of negligence. See Insurance Agent, Insurance Broker, Managing General Agent, and General Agent. See Bailee. See Imputed Negligence. See Subagent.

Agent of Process: One who is authorized to accept service of process on behalf on another. See Process Agent.

Age of Reason: The age at which minors are presumed to be able to act reasonably and understand the consequences of their actions. Generally a minor less than 7 years old is presumed to be incapable of being negligent. Over the age of 14 the minor - - unless otherwise mentally handicapped - - is generally considered to be responsible for their actions. Between the ages of 7 and 14, the minor's accountability is a fact question to be decided via the legal process.

Allegations: The portion of a legal complaint at law that sets forth the specific actions or lack of actions by the defendant which give rise to the lawsuit being brought. See Count.

Allocated Loss Adjustment Expenses/A.L.A.E.: Those costs incurred in the claims investigation and resolution (including legal fees, outside adjuster costs, police report acquisition, expert witness fees, etc.) that can be directly related, and therefore allocated, to a given claim. See Unallocated Loss Adjustment Expenses.

All-Risk Insurance Coverage: A commonly used, and somewhat misleading, term to describe broad forms of insurance coverage, even though such policies contain specific exclusions. See Named Peril Insurance Coverage.

Alternative Risk Transfer: The seeking of insurance type protection by means other than purchasing traditional insurance policies, such as becoming self insured, or risk pooling with other entities of similar type or make up.

A.M. Best Rating: A designation issued by a New Jersey based company, A.M. Best & Company, to designate the financial security and strength of insurance companies.

Amicus curiae (Latin)/Friend of the Court: A party, with strong views on a matter before a court, who petitions to file a brief to plead the merits of one side or the other, even though not directly and/or personally involved in the litigation.

Annuity: The payment of a fixed or calculated periodic payment for a predetermined period of time or for life.

Apparent Authority: The assumption of an ordinarily prudent person that someone, acting as if they had specific authority from another (agency), was indeed authorized to conduct business for that person, even though such specific authority may or may not have been granted. See Expressed Authority. See Ostensible Authority.

Appeal: The right of any party to a lawsuit to refuse to accept the verdict rendered, and to proceed to a higher court for further consideration. See Remand.

Appeal Bond: A bond to cover the cost of appeal, usually for more than the monetary verdict in civil litigation. See Bond, Surety Bond, Fidelity Bond, Performance Bond.

Appearance: In civil legal matters, the coming into court (personally or via a legal representative) to attest to the proceedings for the plaintiff, or to answer the complaint for the defendant. See Notice of Appearance.

Applicant: The injured worker in a Workers' Compensation matter who files an application for adjustment of his claim with the appropriate state or Federal agency having jurisdiction for such matters. See Claimant. See Respondent.

Appraiser: A person who assesses or determines the value of real or personal property. See Adjuster.

Arbitration: A method to resolve disputes, by agreement, without resorting to litigation and normal court proceedings. Instead, the matter is resolved by appointed or agreed upon individuals to hear evidence and render a decision. May be binding, thus allowing no further appeal from the arbitrator's decision, or non-binding, which would allow either party to resort to any other remedy open to them. See Lawsuit. See Mediation. See Trial.

Arbitrator: A person appointed or agreed upon to hear evidence in a dispute not being heard within the court system. See Arbitration.

Assessable Rates: The type of premiums, usually associated with alternative risk and pooling activities, which may be increased during or following the term of the insurance protection, if the original premium amount is insufficient to cover losses, expenses, etc. See Non-assessable Rates.

Assigned Risk: A program found in many states to provide insurance to high risk entities whereby insurance companies agree to accept insurance on individuals or companies which would otherwise not be acceptable under the insurer's underwriting guidelines.

Assignment: The conveying of certain rights and /or obligations, often provided in a contract, from the person who originally had those rights to some other party. See Contract Assignment.

Assumed Reinsurance: That portion of one or more risks accepted by a reinsurer, from the original insurer or ceding company. See Reinsurance. See Ceded Reinsurance.

Assuming Reinsurer: The party or entity that accepts reinsurance coverage on business written by a primary insurer, or ceding reinsurer. See Ceding Reinsurer. See Retrocessionaire.

Assumption Endorsement: A clause within an insurance policy stating that if the carrier becomes insolvent, the insured may collect, directly from any reinsurer of the policy, that amount the reinsurer would have otherwise owed to the ceding company. See Cut-Through Endorsement.

Assumption of Risk: A legal doctrine which states a person may not recover for an injury received when he voluntarily exposes himself to a danger which he knew of, or should have recognized and appreciated.

Assured: The person who is entitled to the protection and benefits provided by the provisions contained in a policy of insurance. See Insured, Ensured, Named Insured, Policyholder.

Attorney: A person who is educated in the law, and who is allowed to represent others in legal and court proceedings. See Lawyer.

Attractive Nuisance: A legal doctrine which states that anyone who owns, creates or maintains an instrument or condition which can reasonably be assumed to be a source of danger to children, must take precautions to prevent injury to children of tender ages who might be attracted to the instrument or condition.

Automobile Insurance: A type of insurance policy which generally insures the drivers' legal liability arising from the use of an insured vehicle, and also may cover the damage to the insured's own vehicle(s) damaged by specific perils.

B

Bad Faith: A violation of the inherent understanding in all contracts and business dealings that all parties to a contract or business arrangement will act toward one another with a sense of good faith and fair dealing. See Good Faith. See Covenant of Good Faith.

Bailee: A person or entity to whom goods are entrusted, but who does not act on behalf of the bailor, and whose negligence is not imputed to the bailor. See Bailor. See Agent. See Imputed Negligence.

Bailment: The delivery of goods or property to a person for that person's benefit, or for mutual benefit of the parties, and which does not convey any responsibility back to the owner of the property for the bailee's actions. See Bailee. See Bailor. See Agency. See Master-Servant Doctrine.

Bailor: One who entrusts his goods to another without conveying any specific instructions, nor controls the actions of the bailee. See Bailee. See Agent.

Bar to Recovery: The term used to describe an action or specific law that will preclude a plaintiff or claimant from collecting any payment for damages that may have resulted from an accident or occurrence.

Bench Trial: A trial wherein there is no jury, and the judge assumes both functions, ruling on matters of law and matters of fact. See Jury Trial. See Trial.

Beneficiary: A person who receives benefits, usually from an insurance policy or other legal directive such as a will or trust. See Third Party Beneficiary.

Betterment: The term used to describe a settlement or replacement of damaged property with other property that is of greater value than that being replaced. In real property matters, the replacement of an older or less useful item with a newer or more costly item. See Depreciation.

Bifurcated Trial: A civil trial in which the issues of liability are tried and ruled on separately and prior to the issues of damages being considered.

Bill of Particulars: The formal rendering of written allegations by one party against another, and also makes a legal demand to have the dispute adjudicated in a court of law. See Complaint.

Binder: An agreement, usually in writing, whereby an insurance company or their representative agrees to issue a policy of insurance before all necessary information is gathered and processed, in effect committing to the coverage before the policy is actually issued.

Blacklisting: The action of predetermining that a person or entity is unacceptable as an insured based on non-insurance related criteria such as race, origin, location of domicile, or other such subjective considerations. See Red Lining.

Bodily Injury: Physical injury to a person, as opposed to psychological trauma, mental anguish, or damage to real or personal property. See Personal Injury.

Bond: A certificate or evidence of a debt, or a promise to pay for a specific purpose. See Appeal Bond/Surety Bond/Fidelity Bond/Performance Bond.

Bordereau: Usually associated with reinsurance writings. A periodic report of premiums, losses, claims expenses, etc., covering a particular cedant or assumed carrier, a specific risk, or a book of business, and showing the applicable amounts and coverage dates of the reinsurance coverage.

Borrowed/Loaned Servant: The legal doctrine which states that if an employer loans a worker to another employer, the employee is considered to be an employee of the borrowing employer in matters such as Workers' Compensation. See Loaned/Borrowed Servant.

Breach of Contract: The failure of one or more parties to adhere to the requirements and agreements of a contract. In an insurance policy, such a breach might jeopardize coverage for a given situation or might void the entire policy.

Broker: An insurance sales person working on a commission basis, and without a contractual agreement with the individual insurance companies with which policies are written. Usually represents the insured or prospective insurance buyer rather than the insurance company. See Agent, Insurance Agent, Insurance Broker, Managing General Agent, General Agent. .

Builders' Risk Coverage: A policy of insurance generally purchased by contractors, and others involved in the building trades, which protects the materials and equipment that belong to the builder while they are at the building site.

Bulk Reserve: An amount of money set aside by an insurance company to pay for estimated losses and related costs, but related to a group of claims rather than to an individual claim. See Reserves, Case Reserves, I.B.N.R. Reserves.

Business Interruption Insurance: A type of insurance that protects the insured from business losses that are sustained as the result of specific types of perils. This type of insurance is aimed at replacing such intangibles as earnings and profits for a business that has suffered a specific type of loss.

Business Invitee: A person on someone's premises by invitation, and usually for the mutual benefit of both parties. See Invitee.

C

Cancellation: The termination, by either the insured or the insurance company, of an insurance policy. See Policy Cancellation.

Captive Insurance Company: An insurance company, usually established and run by and for the benefit of a single insured or group of insureds with common or similar interests. Such insurers may offer their services to the general insuring public, but generally remain focused on the original insured or insureds for which they were created. See Mutual Company, Stock Company, and Reciprocal Company,

Case Reserves: The amount of money set aside by the insurance company, which is estimated to be sufficient to pay for the loss on a given claim. See Reserves/ Loss Reserves.

Casualty Insurance: The type of insurance primarily concerned with providing protection against losses for injury and damage caused by the insured, or for which the insured may have a legal or statutory liability. See Property Insurance.

Catastrophe Loss: A designation assigned to certain types of losses, usually natural in origin, which produces extensive damage to property and/or loss of life, and which represents a significant monetary impact to the insurance coverage written in the area of the catastrophe. For insurance purposes, a specific loss must be designated as a catastrophe by the appropriate insurance bureau. Insurance catastrophes are numbered sequentially, on an annual basis, for identification purposes.

Cedant: The primary or excess insurer that submits a request to a reinsurer for that reinsurer to provide reinsurance on a "blanket" type basis (as in a Reinsurance Treaty arrangement), or on a particular underlying policy (Facultative Reinsurance). See Treaty Reinsurance. See Facultative Reinsurance.

Ceded Reinsurance: That portion of one or more risks passed on by an original insurer or ceding company and accepted by a reinsurer. See Reinsurance. See Assumed Reinsurance.

Ceding Reinsurer: A reinsurance carrier that places part or all of its own assumed reinsurance coverage with another reinsurer. See Assuming Reinsurer. See Retrocessionaire.

Certificate of Insurance: A document issued by the insurance company or their authorized representative that indicates the existence of a specific insurance policy and the general parameters of the coverage such as the policy number, named insured, inception and expiration dates, and limits of liability. A certificate of insurance generally conveys no coverage or insurance protection to the entity to whom the certificate is issued, but only verifies the existence of the coverage as it applies to those insured under the policy itself. See Insurance Certificate.

Certiorari (Latin): Following a verdict or opinion, an order from a higher court to the court that rendered the findings, to present a copy of the decision and trial transcript so that the higher court may rule on the possibility of any irregularities made by the lower court. See Writ of Certiorari.

Charge to the Jury: The directions and instructions given by the judge to the jury at the conclusion of the testimony and evidence phase of a trial, wherein the judge advises the jury on the law that must be considered in their deliberations. See Jury Instructions.

Claim: A demand or assertion for a right or benefit. In insurance, the process whereby an insured and/or a claimant seek the payments set forth in the policy. See Loss.

Claimant: The person or entity that seeks legal remedy from another for perceived damages. See Applicant: See Plaintiff.

Claim File: The physical or electronic compilation of the facts and material related to a claim, maintained by the claims facility investigating the facts of the incident giving rise to the claim.

Claims Made Policy: A contract of insurance that agrees to pay for certain losses that occur during the policy period, and which are also made or presented during the policy period. See Retroactive Coverage. See Occurrence Policy.

Class Action: A means whereby one member of a large group may file suit on behalf of the entire group, if certain circumstances and criteria are met.

Coinsurance Clause: A provision in an insurance policy which limits the liability of the insurer to a proportion of the loss, based on the amount the applicable insurance bears to the value of the property insured. When such a clause exists in a policy, all applicable losses are reduced by this proportionate amount.

Collateral Source Rule: The amount of damages received by a prevailing party cannot be diminished by taking credit for payments made to the plaintiff by some party other than the defendant. The wrong-doer cannot profit from payments made to the plaintiff by other independent sources.

Combined Loss Ratio: The percentage of premium that has been allocated to pay for both loss and loss expense. See Loss Ratio. See Pure Loss Ratio.

Coming to Rest Doctrine: Most automobile insurance policies contain a clause providing liability coverage for situations arising from the loading or unloading of the automobile. Under this doctrine, the loading and unloading activity ceases when that which is being loaded or unloaded comes to rest and the activity is no longer in process.

Commission: The portion of an insurance premium that the agent and/or broker take for their payment in placing the insurance with the carrier.

Common Law: The body of law that is made up of past decisions rendered by the courts, rather than laws enacted by legislative bodies, and upon which decisions may be based in current lawsuits. See Statutory Law. See Equity.

Commutation: The exchanging of certain rights and obligations (often related to future payments owed) for a different set of rights and obligations agreed upon by all parties to the original transaction or agreement. In many instances this involves the buying back of certain future potential indebtedness via a single current payment. See Policy Buy-Back.

Company Surplus: The amount of assets the insurance company owns, less their liabilities. In most states, an insurer's surplus determines the amount of new business (added potential liability) the carrier can write. See Surplus. See Underwriting Surplus.

Comparative Negligence (Pure and Modified): A legal principal which allows for the recovery of a portions of ones damages equal to the proportion the damaged party's own negligence bears to the combined negligence of all parties involved in the accident or occurrence.

Pure Comparative Negligence would allow the damaged party to recoup whatever proportion their damages had to the total negligence, while Modified Comparative Negligence would require the negligence of the damaged party to be less than 50 percent of the total negligence of all involved parties. See Contributory Negligence.

Complaint: The formal rendering of written allegations by one party against another, and also makes a legal demand to have the dispute adjudicated in a court of law. See Lawsuit, also Bill of Particulars

Concurrent Coverage: Two or more applicable insurance policies that provide substantially the same type and scope of coverage for a single accident or occurrence, and which should respond to the claim submitted.

Consideration: The thing of value which one party to a contract agrees to provide to the other party in order to bind the contract and make it a legal document. See Contract.

Contingency Fee: An arrangement whereby a person agrees to perform certain services for payment based on the outcome of those services, rather than on any predetermined rate of compensation.

Contract: A legal document wherein two or more parties agree to perform certain acts for the benefit of one, or the other, or both. The contract process is made up of an offer by one party to do or refrain from doing something, an acceptance of the offer by the other party, and the rendering of something of value — the consideration — to bind the contract.

Contract Assignment: The act of conveying the rights and obligations set forth in a contract, from one entity who is a party to the contract, to another entity, usually not a party to the original contract. See Assignment.

Contract of Adhesion: A contract to which one party agreed because it was the only apparent way in which to receive certain goods and/or services from the other party, but in which the agreeing party had little or no means to bargain or negotiate due to the lack of relative strength of position between the parties. See Adhesion Contract.

Contract Reformation: The act of reframing a contract from it's original wording to encompass new terms, so as to remedy a mistake or lack of equity in the original contract, and better reflect the intent of the parties.

Contractual Coverage: Insurance protection, usually in a General Liability Policy, which provides defense and indemnification for allegations arising from a breech of contractual obligation(s) on the part of the insured. This type of insurance coverage usually does not provide for damages related to "specific performance" of the contract terms, but rather provides for damages related to the contract breech itself.

Contribution: The sharing of a legal responsibility by two or more parties, to provide legal remedy to a damaged or injured party. The right of such contributions among parties is often found in Workers' Compensation laws, and may also be applicable to certain common law issues in some jurisdictions. Conversely, some jurisdictions specifically forbid contribution among joint tort feasors in civil litigation.

Contributory Negligence: Negligence of the damaged party, which contributed in some way to the ultimate damage. In those jurisdictions recognizing this doctrine, it is a complete bar to recovery of any damages. See Comparative Negligence.

Conversion: The unauthorized taking, using, or controlling; i.e., converting, of someone's rights or property for the usurper's own advantage.

Cooperative Insurance Company: A company organized for the purpose of rendering economic services to shareholders or members, generally without financial gain to itself.

Count: In a lawsuit, the plaintiff's statement of his cause of action. A civil complaint may include several counts, each, if considered alone, would constitute a separate allegation against the defendant(s). See Allegations.

Course and Scope of Employment, Arising Out of: The portion of Workers' Compensation law that determines if an injury will be considered as compensable, and as having been encountered while the injured party was performing work related tasks. See Workers' Compensation. See Course of Employment. See Scope of Employment

Course of the Employment: In Workers' Compensation, the injury must come about from an activity directly and naturally resulting from the employee's work duties and responsibilities; i.e., "arising from the course of the work." See Workers' Compensation. See Course and Scope of Employment. See Scope of Employment

Covenant Not To Sue: A document in which the claimant agrees to discharge one or more specific parties to a particular incident, without discharging other known or unknown parties. See General Release.

Covenant of Good Faith and Fair Dealing: The inherent understanding in all contracts and business dealings that all parties to the contract or business arrangement will act toward one another with a sense of good faith and fair dealing. See Bad Faith. See Good Faith.

Coverage: The protection afforded by an insurance policy.

Cross Complaint: A pleading, filed by a defendant in a lawsuit, against the plaintiff who originally brought the lawsuit, alleging the defendant has a claim against the plaintiff in this same matter before the court. This is unlike a Third Party Complaint wherein the defendant files a pleading in order to include in the lawsuit some other entity, not a party to the original suit. See Third Party Complaint.

"Cumis" Counsel: Independent counsel hired by the insured and paid by the insurance company. So named for a California lawsuit in which plaintiff (Cumis) won the right to have personal counsel paid by his carrier. Differs from the defense attorney who is hired by the carrier to represent the personal interests of the insured. Need for independent counsel may arise when certain allegations in the lawsuit pose a potential conflict of interest between insured and insurer: i.e., what is covered and not covered by the insurance contract.

Cumulative Trauma: An injury occurring as a result of continuous type of activity, which by itself as a single incident would not normally cause harm or injury. It is the repetitive nature of the activity, rather than the activity itself, which does the damage. See Repetitive Trauma.

Cut-Through Endorsement: A clause within an insurance policy that provides that if the carrier becomes insolvent, the insured may collect, directly from any reinsurer of the policy, that amount the reinsurer would have otherwise owed to the ceding company. See Assumption Endorsement.

D

"Daily": a colloquial, and now somewhat archaic, term to denote an insurance policy. See Policy.

Damages: The personal, bodily, emotional, or monetary injury suffered as a result of the negligence of someone else. In a law suit, when damages are awarded they may be of various types, such as compensatory damages to reimburse direct loss, special damages which follow as a result of the incident, punitive or exemplary damages assessed to punish the wrongdoer beyond the actual damages sustained, etc.

Dangerous Instrumentality: Anything that has the inherent capacity to place people in peril, either by itself or by careless use.

Declarations Page: One of the sections of an insurance policy that, with the other sections (Insuring Agreement, Exclusions, and Policy Conditions), makes up the generally expected policy format. That section of the policy that usually individualizes the policy form to make it specific as to a particular insured, location, period of time, etc. See Policy Declarations Page.

Declaratory Judgment: A ruling by the court that, as a matter of law, a particular finding is rendered that may prohibit or limit one party's cause of action.

Declaratory Petition: A filing by one party to a lawsuit asking for the judge to rule on a specific legal right of the party, often to determine if the plaintiff has sufficient grounds to bring the action against the defendant.

Deductible: That portion of a loss that the insured agrees to bear on his own without indemnification from the insurer, although the insurer will still adjust the loss from the first dollar. See Self Insured Retention.

Defendant: The person against whom a claim or lawsuit is being brought. See Plaintiff.

Demand for Settlement: In negotiations to finalize a claim or lawsuit, the defendant generally will express willingness to accept certain sums, or certain actions by the plaintiff, in order to end the matter. See Offer of Settlement. See Acceptance of Settlement.

De minimis (*de minimis non curat lex*) (Latin): Of small matter or consequences. Under the law, the doctrine is that the law does not concern itself with small matters.

Demurrer: The response to a lawsuit by the defendant which indicates that even if the allegations being brought against him are true, they are insufficient to sustain the claim, and therefore insufficient for the plaintiff to proceed with the litigation.

Deposition: The rendering of a written statement, usually in the form of questions and answers, by parties to a lawsuit, or others having knowledge of the matters to which the lawsuit pertains. It is administered under oath and has the same weight as court testimony. See Examination Under Oath. See Pre-Trial Activity.

Depreciation: The diminution in value of real property, generally due to age or use. See Betterment.

Directed Verdict: The rendering of a verdict by a judge, as a matter of law, against the party who has the burden of proof, when that burden has not been met. The verdict is generally rendered after the party has presented their evidence and has not established a prima facia case sufficient to be presented to a jury. See Summary Judgment/Nonsuit.

Directors & Officers Insurance: The protection obtained by a corporation to protect itself from acts and actions by members of their Board of Directors and/or the officers of the corporation. The insurance policy is written to protect the corporation, and may or may not provide insurance protection to the individual directors and officers.

Discounted Rate: A premium rate that is reduced from the rate that would otherwise normally be charged for the same protection. The reduction is often arbitrary and related to sales and marketing efforts to attract new business or to hold existing business, or to otherwise be competitive in the marketplace. See Manual Rate.

Discovery: The activity occurring after the filing of a legal action in which the parties are allowed to determine certain facts and obtain certain material to fortify their legal position. In civil litigation, discovery usually includes, but is not limited to, depositions, interrogatories, subpoenas for material, etc. See Pre-Trial Activity.

Dismissal of Action: The action whereby the court of proper jurisdiction closes a matter before it.

Diversity of Citizenship: A doctrine of the Federal Courts that provides jurisdiction by the court over citizens or entities of differing states, or other countries. See Jurisdiction.

Draft: Similar to a check in that it is issued to another for payment, but is not payable until the bank is authorized by the maker to release the funds necessary to honor the instrument.

Also, the initial preparation of a document, subject to possible later changes and/or revisions.

Dram Shop Laws: That body of laws (in some states) which allow a party injured by an intoxicated person operating a motor vehicle to seek damages from the person or entity who served the alcohol to the intoxicated person.

Drop Down Coverage: In a reinsurance contract, this provision ensures that if a lower layer of reinsurance coverage were exhausted, the next higher level would drop down and address the loss as if it had written at that lower level.

Duty (Owed/Violated): In civil law, persons have a duty to act as an ordinarily prudent person would under like or similar circumstances. This is a duty owed by all persons to all others, in general situations. Under certain specific circumstances, some courts have imposed a higher standard (such as on those operating public livery conveyances), or a lower standard of care (such as the duty to trespassers). The owing of a duty and the violation of that duty are generally necessary to show negligence in civil matters. See Negligence. See Proximate Cause. See Liability.

E

Earned Premium: The calculation of the ratio, or percentage, that the total amount of the premium charged for an insurance policy bears to the amount of time lapsed on the policy. It is the premium for that portion of insurance coverage that has been provided during the time the policy has been in effect: i.e., the written premium, less the unearned premium. See Gross Premium. See Net Premium. See Retro-Premium. See Unearned Premium. See Written Premium.

Economic Damages: Those damages which flow from such things as past or future lost wages, loss of value, loss of business, etc.

Employers' Liability Insurance: Insurance designed to protect employers from claims against them brought by their employees, which are not covered by the employer's General Liability policy.

Endorsement: An attachment to an insurance policy that changes or modifies the language, terms, or conditions in the policy itself. See Rider.

Ensured: The person who is entitled to the protection and benefits provided by the provisions contained in a policy of insurance. See Assured, Insured, Named Insured, Policyholder.

Equitable Relief: The rendering of court decisions, from a court with equity powers, based on fairness, rather than prior common law decisions. See Equity.

Equity: The rendering of a court decision, from a court with equity powers, based on fairness, rather than prior common law decisions. See Equitable Relief. See Common Law. See Statutory Law.

Errors & Omissions Coverage: A type of insurance which indemnifies the insured for payments made to others for damages sustained due to a business and/or professional error or oversight committed by the insured.

Escape Clause: Although generally all parties to a contract are bound by the conditions of that contract, and to the "specific performance" called for under that contract, an Escape Clause in the contract would allow one or more of the parties to avoid compliance with the contract terms and conditions, in the event certain things occurred and/or certain conditions were met.

Estoppel: A legal principle that prevents one party from claiming a right he might otherwise have been entitled to, due to his own action or conduct upon which the other party relied. Often used in concert with, but differing from, the term "waiver": See Waiver. See Imputed Negligence.

Examination Under Oath: The rendering of a statement, usually in the form of questions and answers, by parties to a lawsuit or others having knowledge of the matters to which the lawsuit pertains. It is administered under oath and has the same weight as court testimony. See Deposition.

Excess and Surplus Lines Broker: A seller of insurance policies, specifically licensed to provide coverage when traditional or normally existing insurance markets are not available. The Excess and Surplus Lines policies are usually provided from "non-admitted" insurance carriers. See Admitted Insurance Company. See Non-admitted Insurance Company. See Surplus Lines.

Excess Insurance: Insurance coverage which is written to come into effect only after certain specified underlying policy coverages have been exhausted by payment; or, in some circumstances, when the underlying coverages do not apply to a particular loss. See Umbrella Policy.

Exclusion: In an insurance policy, a clause that, under certain circumstances, eliminates and/or limits coverage otherwise granted within the policy. See Exclusion Section. See Policy Exclusions.

Exclusion Section (of Insurance Policy): One of the sections of an insurance policy that, with the other sections (Declarations Page, Insuring Agreement, and Policy Conditions) makes up the generally accepted policy format. That provision in an insurance policy that limits or eliminates coverage for certain specific items, instances, or circumstances spelled out in the provision. See Exclusion. See Policy Exclusions.

Exclusive Remedy (Workers' Compensation): That portion of the Workers' Compensation laws that states an employee, injured in the course and scope of his employment and therefore eligible for Workers' Compensation benefits, may not choose a common law remedy which might otherwise be available to him to seek damages for his injury, but may only avail himself of the sole remedy provided under the applicable Workers' Compensation laws.

Exemplary Damages: Damages awarded to the plaintiff, over and above the judgment for the actual loss, and assessed as a punishment to the defendant for egregious conduct such as fraud, malice, or wanton conduct. See Punitive Damages. See Extra Contractual Damages.

Ex Gratia Payment: A payment made by an insurer (usually to their insured) that is not required under the provisions of the applicable insurance policy, but rather for marketing or "good will" purposes.

Expense Reserves: The amount of money set aside by the insurance company to pay for allocated loss adjustment expenses related to a claim. See Case Reserves. See I.B.N.R. Reserve. See Loss Reserve. See Reserve.

Experience Rating: The calculating of an insurance premium based on the past loss experience of the specific insured, rather than a rate based on a general class of like or similar risks.

Expert Witness: A person called to testify at a legal proceeding in which the person has some extraordinary level of knowledge, experience and expertise, and who can render opinions and facts for the judge and jury to assist them in making a final judgment of the issues. See Lay Witness.

Expiration Date: The date that coverage under an insurance policy ends. The last date for which coverage is in effect. Under a Claims Made Policy, this would be the date by which a claim would have to be incurred and reported to the insurer. In an Occurrence Policy, claims would still be viable if the occurrence took place prior to the expiration date, even if it was not reported by that time to the insurer. See Claims Made Policy. See Inception date. See Occurrence Policy.

Exposure/Insurance Risk: The risk assumed by an insurance company or self-insured organization when it agrees to offer coverage.

Exposure Modifier: In Workers' Compensation premium calculations, the modification or adjustment of the basic (or general class) premium, to reflect an increase or decrease in that basic premium, due to a higher or lower than expected frequency of claims, and/or a higher or lower than expected severity of injuries. See "X Mod."

Expressed Authority: That specifically assigned right which empowers someone to act in a particular way, usually on behalf of another, as in an agency relationship. See Agency. See Ostensible Authority.

Extra Contractual Damages: Damages in a judgment or settlement that are outside the scope of the insurance policy. See Exemplary Damages. See Punitive Damages.

F

Facultative Reinsurance: Reinsurance coverage that is secured by a ceding company via a submission of a cedant's specific policy to the reinsurer, and a request for reinsurance limits, specific layers of coverage, etc., on that specific risk. See Treaty Reinsurance.

Family Purpose Doctrine: A law adhered to in some states and jurisdictions which holds that the owner of an automobile may be held responsible for the negligence of another family member operating that car, even though the operating family member is not in an agency relationship with the owner: i.e., not acting on behalf of the owner. See Agency.

Federal Rules of Civil Procedure: Those rules that govern civil litigation in U.S. District Courts, and after which most state court rules are modeled.

Fidelity Bond: A bond covering potential losses from employees or fiduciaries due to embezzlement, larceny, or gross negligence. See Appeal Bond. See Bond. See Performance Bond. See Surety Bond,

Fidelity Insurance: A type of insurance policy that agrees to reimburse an insured for losses caused by the dishonesty of an officer, employee, agent, or fiduciary of the insured.

Fiduciary: A person or entity that manages money or property for another and who must exercise a standard of care to act primarily for the other's benefit.

Filing Complaint: The act of registering the formal bill of particulars, which constitutes a lawsuit, with the court having jurisdiction to hear the matter. Such an action will prevent the tolling of the statute of limitations for filing such a lawsuit: however, it will not activate the litigation process further until a copy of the complaint is served on the defendant to the action. See Statute of Limitations. See Serving the Complaint.

First Party: In insurance matters, the insured party. For insurance claims, the person making claim under their own policy for injury or loss suffered by the person or property being insured. See Third Party.

Force Majeure (Latin): A superior or irresistible force, outside the control of the parties, such as an act of God, which keeps a contract or other such action from being completed.

Forum Shopping: An attempt to find a jurisdiction for legal action that is more favorable than another jurisdiction.

Fronting Company: An insurance company which issues a policy, and thereby appears to the world to be the insurer, but which has passed on to other insurers or reinsurers, some or all of the risk of the coverage.

G

G.A.A.P (Generally Accepted Accounting Principles): Rules and procedures that are generally accepted by most, if not all, aspects of the business community as they relate to accounting practices.

General Agent: A person or entity engaged in the insurance agency business, and with whom an insurer has entered into a special arrangement whereby the general agent performs a number of tasks and responsibilities usually performed by the insurance company, such as underwriting, claims adjustment, loss control, policy issuance, etc. See Managing General Agent. See Insurance Agent. See Insurance Broker.

General Release: A document in which the claimant agrees to discharge all parties to a particular incident regardless of whether they were parties to a claim or suit brought by the claimant, or even if they are unknown to the claimant. See Covenant Not To Sue. See Release of Liability Form.

"Going and Coming" Rule: That principle of Workers' Compensation law which indicates that certain employees, by the nature of their work activities, are to be considered as being in the course and scope of their employment while going to or coming from their place of employment. See Workers' Compensation.

Good Faith: The inherent understanding in all contracts and business dealings that all parties to the contract or business arrangement will act toward one another with a sense of good faith and fair dealing. See Bad Faith. See Covenant of Good Faith.

Gross Premium: The amount charged for insurance coverage, including the added amount calculated to cover the anticipated expenses and profit margin for the policy term. See Earned Premium. See Net Premium. See Premium. See Written Premium.

Guardian Ad Litem (Latin): A person appointed to act on behalf of another because the true party in interest is a minor or otherwise incapacitated. See ad litem.

H

Hazard: That which causes or increases a risk and/or the possibility of a loss. See Peril. See Risk.

Hold Harmless Agreement: A contract clause whereby one party agrees to assume the liability of another. See Indemnification Agreement. See Save Harmless Clause.

Homeowner's Insurance: A type of insurance policy that combines property insurance on the dwelling and contents with casualty insurance to protect the owner and/or occupier from personal liability.

I

Implead: To add a previously unnamed party to an existing lawsuit on the basis that the party being joined may be liable to one or more of the parties already in the litigation.

Implied Authority: The rights of an agent to act on behalf of the principal, even though the specific right(s) are not set forth or specified in advance. The reasoning behind such actions lies in the fact that such authority is usual and common in this type of relationship.

Imputed Negligence: Negligence of one party that is chargeable to another under certain situations, as when a principal is held accountable for the negligence of his agent. See Agency. See Agent. See Bailee. See Estoppel. See Negligence. See Respondeat Superior.

In Camera (Latin): Legal proceedings or specific court activities conducted in the private chambers of the judge and away from spectators, the jury, media, etc.

Inception date: The date on which coverage begins under a policy of insurance. See Expiration Date.

Incorporation: The act of forming a legal entity with perpetual existence, which protects those who own shares in said corporation from personal responsibility for liability imposed on the corporate body. See "Piercing the Corporate Veil".

Incurred But Not Reported (IBNR): An actuarial estimate of the amount of money needed to pay for claims and associated costs of future losses that have occurred but have not yet been reported to the insurer. These estimates are based on the type and severity of similar cases already reported to the insurance company. See Bulk

Reserves. See Case Reserves. See Loss Reserves. See Reserves.

Incurred Loss: A loss that has occurred, but which has not yet been resolved. Also, in calculating claims experience, the total of all payments on a given claim or claims, plus the remaining loss reserves on that claim or claims. See Reserves. See Incurred But Not Reported (IBNR).

Indemnification: Holding one person responsible for the damages caused by another's actions, due to the first party having agreed to do so.

Indemnification Agreement: A contract clause whereby one party agrees to pay the damages for which another party may be held responsible. See Hold Harmless Agreement. See Save Harmless Clause.

Indemnity: The act of one person agreeing to be responsible for the damages resulting from another person's acts or actions.

Independent Adjuster: A person offering his services for hire to investigate and possibly settle an insurance claim on behalf of another. Usually such persons represent the insurance company. See Public Adjuster.

Injunction: A court ruling issued in equity that prohibits the activities of one party, and restrains the party from taking certain specific action(s). The ruling does not generally relate to the question of alleged money damages. See Injunctive Relief.

Injunctive Relief: The filing with the court a petition to grant one party specific relief from the acts or actions of another party. These filings are generally related to matters of equity rather than money damages. See Injunction.

Inland Marine Coverage: Originally a term to describe insurance on goods being transported by means other than by ocean going ships. It has been expanded to encompass many sub-types of coverages to include insurance on specified personal articles such as jewelry under a Homeowner's policy or goods held by a bailee. See Marine Coverage.

Insurable Interest: In matters of insurance, the principle that demands the person acquiring insurance on another person, or piece of property, or activity, must have some legally recognized interest in that insured person, property or activity.

Insurance: An agreement whereby, for a stipulated consideration, one party agrees to compensate the other for losses sustained in the event certain things occur.

Insurance Agent: A person or entity that sells insurance on behalf of one or more insurance companies. See Insurance Broker

Insurance Broker: An insurance sales person working on a commission basis, and without a contractual agreement with the insurance companies with which the policy is written. Usually represents the insured or prospective insurance buyer rather than the insurance company. See Agent. See General Agent. See Insurance Agent. See Insurance Broker. See Managing General Agent,

Insurance Capacity: The amount of insurance a company may write, in addition to what they have already written, while still being able to maintain the financial balance and stability imposed by various governing bodies that regulate the insurance industry.

Insurance Certificate: A document issued by the insurance company or their authorized representative that indicates the existence of a specific insurance policy, and the general parameters of the coverage such as the policy number, named insured, inception and expiration dates, and limits of liability. A certificate of insurance generally conveys no coverage or insurance protection to the entity to whom the certificate is issued, but only verifies the existence of the coverage as it applies to those insured under the policy itself. See Certificate of Insurance.

Insured: The person or entity that is being protected under a policy of insurance. See Assured. See Ensured. See Insurable Interest. See Named Insured. See Policyholder.

Insurer: The company or person that is providing the insurance.

Insuring Agreement: One of the sections of an insurance policy that, with the other sections (Declarations Page, Exclusions, and Policy Conditions), makes up the usual policy format. That section of the policy in which are usually found the parameters of what type of insurance is being provided, the property being insured, the perils being covered, etc.

Intentional Acts: Actions that are non-fortuitous and come about by the purposeful or designed actions of someone. Damages arising from intentional acts are generally not covered by insurance, and rendered as punitive in nature. See Exemplary Damages. See Extra Contractual Damages. See Punitive Damages. See Public Policy.

Interinsurance Exchange (also Reciprocal Insurance Company): A group or association of persons cooperating through an attorney in fact, for the purpose of insuring themselves and each other. See Captive Insurance Companies. See Mutual Insurance Company. See Stock Insurance Company. See Reciprocal Exchange.

Interlocking Clause: The wording in a reinsurance contract that indicates the payment of a loss will be apportioned between reinsurers if there is more than one reinsurance contract in effect covering the loss.

Interrogatories: A set of questions posed by one party to a lawsuit to be answered by one or more other parties to the same litigation. The answers are rendered under oath, and carry the same weight as testimony rendered at trial. See Pre-trial Activity.

Intervening Act: An act that takes place after the act that gave rise to an action (the negligence) and before the resulting damage, and which alters the ultimate result of that initial negligent act. Generally it is such that the original wrongdoer could not have anticipated this intervening act to have occurred in the normal course of event. See Last Clear Chance. See Supervening Negligence.

Inverse Condemnation: An action to recover, from a governmental agency, the cost of property seized by that agency for the agency's own use or disposition.

Invitee: A person on someone's premises by invitation, and usually for the mutual benefit of both parties. See Business Invitee.

Issues of Fact: Those questions in legal proceedings that relate to what happened in a specific instance, and that can be proven by testimony of the parties and/or witnesses. In litigation, issues of fact are decided by the jury.

Issues of Law: Those questions in legal proceedings that relate to the body of legislative or common law, and are ruled on by the judge based on the dictates of the particular law or statute.

J

Joint and Severable Liability: Legal responsibility that attaches to one or more parties to a contract such as an insurance policy. The concept allows a plaintiff to sue a single party for their negligence and resultant liability, or to proceed against all parties collectively who may be responsible. See Several Liability.

Joint Tort Feasor: Refers to two or more persons jointly or severally liable for the same injury to a person or property. See Tort Feasor.

Jones Act: A Federal law that allows for persons injured while working aboard a ship to file a claim and/or bring a lawsuit against the owner, master or other crewmembers. In certain circumstances, a longshoreman/stevedore may find relief under this statute if injured while on board the vessel rather than on the dock during a loading or unloading operation. See Longshoremen's and Harbor Workers Act. See Maintenance and Cure.

Judgment: The official court ruling upon the rights or claims of the parties to litigation heard by the court. See Satisfaction of Judgment.

Judgment N.O.V. (Judgment Not Withstanding the Verdict): A judgment entered by the court in favor of one party, even though a verdict has been entered by a jury in favor of the other party.

Jurisdiction: A term denoting the authority of a court to hear certain matters and to render judgments therein. See Venue.

Jurist: Someone schooled and distinguished in the law, usually referring to a judge.

Juror Challenges (Peremptory/For Cause): The right of the attorneys in a legal proceeding to ask the judge to have a juror dismissed from sitting on the jury. Peremptory challenges may be made without offering a specific reason to have the juror dismissed. Challenges for Cause are those in which the prospective juror has an obvious interest or bias in the outcome of a trial. There is generally no limit to the number of challenges for cause.

Jury: A group of the defendant's peers, chosen to hear evidence in a trial, and render a judgment.

Jury Instructions: A set of admonitions and directions given by the judge to the members of a jury before they begin deliberations, usually outlining the matters of law and directing them as to specific findings if certain decisions are made by the jury members. See Charge to the Jury.

Jury Trial: A trial in which one party or another exercises their right to have a panel of peers selected to hear testimony, consider evidence, and render a verdict in favor of one or more parties to the lawsuit. See Bench Trial. See Trial.

L

Laches (Latin): The unreasonable delay by one party to a lawsuit in asserting their rights, and in doing so having placed the other party at a disadvantage. A ruling based on Laches will result in a dismissal of the claim even if the statute of limitations has not yet run. See Statute of Limitations.

Last Clear Chance Doctrine: The legal principle which forgives the actions of an individual who, under other circumstances might be considered negligent, when those actions arose from the individual attempting to avoiding an accident by taking evasive action, and in so doing caused some other tort. Usually only applies in civil automobile damage cases, and is not recognized in all jurisdictions. See Intervening Cause. See Supervening Negligence.

Lawsuit: The method whereby one party brings a legal action against another, requesting that a court of law resolve specific matters in dispute. See Arbitration / Mediation. See Complaint. See Bill of Particulars.

Lawyer: A person who is educated in the law, and who is allowed to represent others in legal and court proceedings. See Attorney.

Lay Witness: A person called to testify at a legal proceeding who has no extraordinary expertise in the matter(s) at hand, but rather is called to testify as to what occurred and what was seen, heard, etc. See Expert Witness.

Lease: As a noun, a contract (usually written) between the owner of certain property (the "lessor") and one or more people (the "lessee") who wish to have or use the property for a definite or indeterminate period of time. The lessee will generally pay the lessor an agreed fee (usually periodically) for said use. See Rent.

As a verb, the act of acquiring (by the lessee) and/or conveying (by the lessor) temporary possession of property for a specific purpose such as housing, business use, etc.

Letter of Credit: A document issued by a financial institution that promises access to certain funds for the person to whom it is issued. It allows added financial liquidity and stability without actually borrowing the funds until needed.

Liability: The legal concept of one person being responsible under the law to another for the results of the first person's actions. Under civil law, a person who has a duty to do something or refrain from doing something, and violates that duty, would be negligent. If that negligence were the proximate cause of injury or damage to another, the party at fault (negligent) would be liable. See Duty. See Negligence. See Proximate Cause. See Tort.

Libel: The defamation of another through printed material, pictures, etc. See Slander.

Liberalization Clause: A section of some insurance policies that indicates if, due to civil verdict, legislative enactment, or other legal precedent, the coverage provided in the policy at issue is more restrictive than what has been determined it should be, the policy will automatically be broadened to encompass the more liberal interpretation.

Lien: An encumbrance placed on property so as to insure the owner of the property pays certain debts.

Limits of Liability: In an insurance policy, the maximum amount of money the insurer will pay under the circumstances as set forth in the policy. The amount of the policy coverage(s).

Liquidated Damages: The amount of damages agreed to by the parties before any actual damages occur so as to eliminate estimates and negotiation of said damages at a later date. Often found in contracts and bonds as the measure of damages if one of the parties defaults or otherwise fails to perform.

Liquor Liability: The legal right of a party to sue not only an automobile driver under the influence of alcohol, but also the person or establishment which served the alcohol to the driver, if the person serving the alcohol knew, or should have known, the person being served was already inebriated.

Loaned/Borrowed Servant: The legal doctrine which states that if an employer loans a worker to another employer, with the workers agreement, the loaned person is considered to be an employee of the borrowing employer in matters such as Workers' Compensation. See Borrowed/Loaned Servant.

Locus (Latin): The place where an incident/accident took place. The location of the loss.

Long Arm Statute: A legislative process whereby legal service may be obtained on a person, company, or other entity that is not a resident of the state, so long as that person, company or entity is doing business, or has other dealing, in the state. See Serving a Complaint.

Longshoreman's' and Harbor Workers' Act: A United States Federal law which provides Workers' Compensation type benefits to employees injured in the course and scope of their employment on navigable waters, and who would therefore not be eligible for individual state mandated Workers' Compensation benefits. An injured worker covered under this Federal Act may still file a lawsuit against a vessel owner under the Jones Act. See Workers' Compensation. See Jones Act. See Maintenance and Cure.

Loss: The event that precipitates the possibility of a claim under an insurance policy. See Claim.

Loss Adjustment Expense: The costs of investigating, adjusting, and litigating a claim, other than the costs associated with actually paying the loss.

Loss Development: The calculation of the gross incurred loss in a policy, class of business, insured or insurer, from one period of time to another. It is measured by determining the new reserves established during this time frame, plus reserve increases on previously reserved cases that remain open, minus any decreases on previously reserved cases still open, plus or minus any difference between payments and reserves on cases closed during this period. A positive Loss Development figure is considered to be "unfavorable", while a negative Loss Development figure is "favorable."

Loss Payable Clause: A portion of an insurance policy that provided that any settlement under the policy will be made either to the entity named in the clause, or jointly to the insured and the entity named in the clause. It protects the insurance interest of someone other than the insured, usually such as a mortgagor, or owner of the property.

Loss Payee: The entity named in an insurance policy that will be paid, individually or jointly with the insured, in the event of a loss to the property being insured. Such an entity is generally not an insured, and therefore receives no specific coverage protection other than their financial interest in the property designated. The Loss Payee is usually a mortgagor, lien holder, or true owner of the property who has an insurable interest along with the insured.

Loss Ratio: The percentage of insurance premiums allocated to the payment of loss and/or loss expense. See Combined Loss Ratio. See Pure Loss Ratio.

Loss Reserve: The amount of money set aside by the insurance company to pay for known and/or unknown claims, exclusive of associated costs for expenses. See Case Reserves. See Expense Reserve. See I.B.N.R. See Reserve.

M

Maintenance and Cure: Under the Federal laws governing seamen and stevedores injured while working aboard a ship, the injured individual is entitled to "maintenance and cure" from his injuries. See Workers' Compensation. See Longshoreman's and Harbor Worker's Act. See Jones Act.

Malpractice: Professional actions and/or conduct that falls below the acceptable standard of care.

Managing General Agent: A person or entity engaged in the insurance agency business, and with whom an insurer has entered into a special arrangement whereby the general agent performs a number of tasks and responsibilities usually performed by the insurance company, such as underwriting, claims adjustment, loss control, policy issuance, etc. A Managing General Agent may also be engaged in the control and/or supervision of other agencies on behalf of the insurer. See General Agent. See Insurance Agent. See Insurance Broker.

Manual Rate: The insurance premium rate at which a risk is expected to be profitable to the insurer. These are usually "published" rates that the underwriters may reduce to be more competitive in the marketplace. See Discounted Rate.

Marine Coverage: Insurance protection against certain perils generally and primarily associated with risks at sea, and usually covering the ship itself, the freight, and cargo. Also referred to as Ocean Marine Coverage although it may be written to cover water transportation risks in navigable waterways other than the oceans. See Inland Marine Coverage.

Master-Servant Doctrine: The legal premise that holds the principle (master) accountable for the acts of the servant (agent) if those actions are being performed for the master's benefit. This relationship exists in an employer-employee relationship so long as the employer (master) is directing the work and activities of the employee (servant.) See Agency. See Bailment.

Mistrial: The cessation of a trial without a verdict being rendered because of some extraordinary event that is prejudicial to one or more of the parties and which, in the judge's opinion, cannot be corrected if the trial continues.

Modified Comparative Negligence: See Comparative Negligence.

Motion: A legal brief or statement, on behalf of one of the parties to a lawsuit, that asks the court to consider certain facts or action, and to render a decision based on the arguments made. See Pre Trial Activity. See Motion in Limine.

Motion in Limine: A written motion, usually prepared before a trial begins, with the intent of precluding or limiting certain information from being introduced on the basis that the material or evidence would be prejudicial. See Motion. See Pre-Trial Activity.

Mutual Insurance Company: A company owned by the policyholders, in which profits are distributed to the insured/owners by way of dividends based on the amount their individual premiums compared to the total premiums written. See Stock Company, Reciprocal Company, and Captive Company.

Mysterious Disappearance: The loss of an insured article from a known place without any evidence of theft, and without any credible explanation other than theft for its being gone.

N

Named Insured: The party whose name appears on the Declarations Page of an insurance policy, and who is considered to be the primary insured under the policy. See Assured. See Ensured. See Insured. See Policyholder.

Named Peril Insurance Coverage: The specification within a policy of insurance that only certain enumerated causes of loss will be considered to be covered under the policy in question. See All Risk Insurance Coverage.

Navigable Waters: A body of water that by itself, or in connection with one or more other bodies of water, forms passage over which commerce may be undertaken by water vessels.

Negligence: In civil matters, the violation of a duty to do something or refrain from doing something. The types of duty owed may vary depending on the relationships of the parties, and the circumstances giving rise to a legal action. See Duty. See Liability. See Proximate Cause. See Standard of Care.

Negligent Entrustment: A theory of legal liability wherein the liable party did not commit the direct act(s) causing injury and/or damage to the plaintiff, but rather was guilty of providing, or allowing the usage of, an instrument by another party whom the first party knew or should have known was incompetent to operate or use the instrument in question.

Net Premium: The amount charged for insurance coverage, not including any added amount calculated to cover the anticipated expenses and profit margin for the policy term. See Gross Premium. See Premium.

Niche Market: A section of the economy where there is a specific need for certain goods or services, but which is not being provided by the general sellers or purveyors in that area.

No Fault Insurance: A type of insurance in which claims for personal injury, and (in some cases) property damage, are made against the claimant's own insurance company rather than against the person at fault. The damages are paid based on the loss sustained without considerations of negligence.

***Nolo Contendere*:(Latin) ("I will not contest it."):** A plea entered by the defendant which generally has the same effect as a guilty plea in terms of court judgment, but which is not entered as an admission of guilt.

Non-admitted Insurance Company: One which is not licensed in a particular state, but nevertheless is legally able to issue insurance policies in that state so long as the type of insurance being written is not available from other admitted carriers. See Admitted Company.

Non-assessable Rates: The type of insurance premiums that are not subject to increases during or following the time for which insurance protection exists. See Assessable Rates.

Non-insurable Risk: A risk that cannot be calculated as to value, potential loss, etc., and is therefore unable to be insured. See Uninsurable Risk

Nonsuit: A term used to indicate the termination of a lawsuit without a finding that is based on the merits of the case. See Directed Verdict. See Summary Judgment.

Non-Waiver Agreement: A document signed by all applicable parties that the actions of the parties to the agreement shall not constitute a waiver of any rights the said parties might have or acquire. See Reservation of Rights.

Notice of Appearance: In civil legal matters, the filing with the court of a document that confirms the parties have appeared and have placed themselves under the direction of the court. See Appearance.

Notice to Appear: The document whereby the court has ordered the defendant in a civil legal matter to appear before that court. Failure to appear will result in a judgment being entered against said defendant. See Summons.

N.O.V. (non obstante veredicto): A court entered judgment in favor of one of the parties to a lawsuit, even though the jury has already entered a judgment in favor of the other party. This overturns the jury verdict. See Verdict N.O.V.

Novation: The exchange of one obligation for another. In insurance, this is the canceling of an existing policy, usually back to it's original inception date regardless of when the novation takes place. It usually involves the payment of some agreed upon amount paid to the policyholder for the cessation of coverage as if it had never existed. This differs from a commutation, which generally ceases coverage for existing and future obligations under the policy, but is not "retro-active" to the inception date. See Commutation. See Policy Buy-Back.

O

Occupational Disease/Occupational Injury: A disease or injury which comes about as a result of a worker's employment, and one which is usually covered by Workers' Compensation laws.

Occurrence: A continuous or repeated exposure to conditions that results in damage or injury. See Accident.

Occurrence Policy: A contract of insurance that agrees to pay for certain losses covered by the policy that occur during the period when the policy is in effect, regardless of when those claims may be made or presented. See Claims Made Policy.

Of Counsel: An attorney involved, on behalf of a party to a lawsuit, but who is not the attorney of record.

Offer of Settlement: In negotiations, to finalize a claim or lawsuit, the plaintiff generally will express willingness to pay certain sums, or to take certain actions, in order to end the matter. See Acceptance of Settlement. See Demand For Settlement.

Omnibus Clause: In an automobile liability insurance policy, this extends coverage to anyone operating the vehicle with the permission of the owner.

Ostensible Authority/Ostensible Agency: The appearance that someone has a specific authority to act in a particular way, which may or may not be an expressed authority. The actions gain credence from the manner, demeanor, or trappings of the person exercising the action(s), whether arising from real or imaginary authority. See Apparent Authority. See Expressed Authority.

"Other Insurance" Clause: One of the conditions in an insurance policy that attempts to deal with the allocation of applicable coverage when more than one insurance policy applies to the same loss. See Policy Conditions.

Over-insured: The condition that exists when there is more insurance on a particular piece of property than the property is worth. This is usually inadvertent and, depending on policy conditions, will generally result in collecting less than policy limits, even for a total loss. See Under Insured.

P

Pain & Suffering: The generic term used to describe the damages paid to an injured party in a civil claim or lawsuit for those intangibles related to the agony and discomfort from their injury.

Paralegal: A person with certain legal skills and experience, but who is not an attorney, who works on legal matters as an assistant to a licensed attorney.

Parol Evidence: Oral or verbal evidence.

Pecuniary: Relating to money, monetary matters, or those things that have monetary value.

Peremptory Challenge: The right of a trial attorney to have a prospective juror removed from the jury without stating a specific reason for the dismissal. See Juror Challenge.

Performance Bond: A bond that protects against loss due to the inability or refusal of a contractor to perform his contract. See Appeal Bond. See Bond. See Fidelity Bond. See Surety Bond,

Peril: That which causes or increases the possibility of a loss or possible loss. See Risk. See Hazard.

Permanent Disability: A physical restriction or limitation in bodily use or function resulting from an injury or disease.

A benefit under Workers' Compensation laws that provides an injured worker, who sustains a compensable injury resulting in some degree of permanent physical or mental impairment, with a settlement to compensate the worker for his restricted future earning capability. See Temporary Disability/Workers' Compensation.

Permissive Use: The right to operate an automobile, given by the owner of that automobile to another person. See Omnibus Clause.

Personal Articles Floater: A type of insurance coverage usually attached to another type of policy such as a Homeowners policy, which provides specific coverage for identified items against individual specified perils, or a broad range of general perils.

Personal Injury: A term somewhat broader than bodily injury and encompassing, in addition, such matters as defamation, slander, libel, etc. See Bodily Injury.

"Piercing the Corporate Veil": A method whereby the normal protection from personal responsibility by the owner of a corporation for liability imposed on the corporation may be circumvented. If the courts feel the act of incorporation was merely to shield the owner from such responsibility, the "veil" of incorporation may be "pierced", thus rendering the owner of the corporation personally responsible for the corporation's liability. See Incorporation.

Plaintiff: The person bringing a claim or lawsuit against another. See Applicant. See Claimant. See Defendant.

Pleadings: The formal written assertions by the parties to a lawsuit that set forth the allegations of the plaintiffs and the defenses of the defendants.

Policy: The contract of insurance between an insurer and an insured. See "Daily".

Policy Buy-Back: The process whereby an insurer (or reinsurer) pays the insured (or cedant) a sum of money to, in effect, cancel the policy as to future payments (both indemnity and expense), including losses incurred but not yet resolved (open reserves). See Commutation.

Policy Cancellation: The termination, by either the insured or the insurance company, of an insurance policy. See Cancellation. See Short Rate Cancellation.

Policy Conditions: One of the sections of an insurance policy that, with the other sections (Declarations Page, Insuring Agreement, and Exclusions), makes up the generally expected policy format. That section of the policy in which the broad rules and regulations governing the specifics in the policy are found.

Policy Declarations Page: One of the sections of an insurance policy that, with the other sections (Insuring Agreement, Exclusions, and Policy Conditions), makes up the generally expected policy format. That section of the policy that usually individualizes the policy form to make it specific as a particular insured, location, period of time, etc. See Declarations Page.

Policy Exclusions: One of the sections of an insurance policy that, with the other sections (Declarations Page, Insuring Agreement, and Policy Conditions), makes up the generally expected policy format. Those provisions in an insurance policy that limit or eliminate coverage for certain specific items, instances, or circumstances spelled out in the provision. See Exclusions. See Exclusion section.

Policy Expiration Date: The last date on which the insurance under a particular policy is in effect.

Policy Inception Date: The first date on which the insurance under a particular policy is in effect.

Policyholder: The party whose name appears on the Declarations Page of an insurance policy, and who is considered to be the primary insured under the policy. See Assured. See Ensured. See Insured. See Named Insured.

Policyholder's Dividends: In mutual insurance companies, the return of certain moneys to policyholders if the company was profitable during the policy period.

Policy Lapse: The ending of the applicable policy coverage either because the time of the policy period has ended, or because the policy has been allowed to expire in mid-term through the failure to pay owed premiums, or for other such requirement.

Policy Period: The time that an insurance policy is in effect, from the inception date to the expiration date. See Policy Expiration Date. See Policy Inception Date.

Policy Reformation: The changing of an entire policy, after it's inception date, when the changes are so broad or sweeping as to make it impractical to revise the contract wording through the use of policy additions or endorsements. See Reformation.

Policy Reinstatement: The act of reactivating a policy which has lapsed or been canceled.

Policy Renewal: The act of continuing a policy of insurance for another policy term, after the previous term has expired.

Prayer: In civil litigation, the term used to describe what the plaintiff is seeking from the defendant. The request contained in a civil complaint for certain monetary or non-monetary relief from the defendant in favor of the plaintiff.

Premium: The amount of money charged by an insurance company to assume all or part of a risk inherent in a policy of insurance. See Earned Premium. See Gross Premium. See Net Premium. See Retro-premium. See Written Premium.

Preponderance of the Evidence: In civil litigation, the burden of proof on the plaintiff is to establish the liability of the defendant based on the weight of the evidence presented. This concept allows the judge or jury to consider or discard any or all of the evidence, and ascribe to it whatever weight seems appropriate. See Reasonable Doubt.

Presumption: The accepting of a fact without proof, until such time as other evidence disproves that acceptance.

Pre-Trial Activity: Following the filing of a legal action such as a law suit, but before the matter actually comes to trial, the parties are allowed to conduct certain activities to bolster their legal position. These activities may include the filing of motions with the court to have certain matters of law changed or ruled on prior to the factual matter being resolved. This may also include taking statements from the parties or witnesses (Depositions), filing lists of questions for the opposing party to answer (Interrogatories), or serving of subpoenas to obtain material bearing on the case, (Subpoena Ducus Takem.) See Deposition. See Discovery. See Interrogatory. See Motion.

Prima Facie: (Latin): Literally means "At first sight." A matter or fact that is presumed to be true until such time that other evidence is introduced to disprove the assumption of truth.

Prior Acts Coverage: Insurance protection purchased to cover the time prior to, and up to, inception of a Claims Made Policy. See "Tail" Coverage.

Privity of Contract: The requirement that there must be some direct relationship between the parties to a contract in order for one party to bring legal action against the other, under the terms of the contract. In many jurisdictions this is no longer the rule of law.

Process Agent: One who is authorized to accept service of process on behalf of another. See Agent of Process.

Producer: The person or entity that sells an insurance policy, such as an insurance agent or insurance broker. See Agent. See Broker. See Insurance Agent. See Insurance Broker.

Product Liability: The legally imposed responsibility of a manufacturer for damage to others caused by the manufacturer's product. In some jurisdictions, this may also be imposed on those who sell, distribute, or are otherwise in the "stream of commerce" for the product. See Products Insurance.

Products Insurance: Coverage for damage or injury caused by a product manufactured or sold by the insured. See Product Liability.

Professional Liability Policy: Insurance coverage for the professional acts or omissions of the insured.

Proffer: To offer a document or other material as evidence.

Proof of Loss: The formal rendering, in writing, of damages and costs as evidence of a claim by a damaged party.

Property Damage: Physical harm, destruction or diminished value of real or personal property.

Property Insurance: The type of insurance usually written to protect the property of the insured against named or general perils. See Casualty Insurance.

Pro Rata Clause: As found in some insurance policies, the clause indicates that any settlement under the policy will only pay a pro rata share of the loss, based on the percentage that the limits of the policy in question bear to the entire amount of coverage available to the insured under all applicable policies.

Pro Se (Latin): Appearing on one's own behalf rather than being represented by an attorney.

Proximate Cause: An act or acts in an unbroken and continuous chain of events that causes injury or damage that would not have otherwise occurred. See Liability.

Public Adjuster: A person offering his services for hire to investigate, and possibly settle, an insurance claim on behalf of another. Usually such persons represent the insured in their claim against the insurance company. See Independent Adjuster.

Public Policy: In legal actions which result in the rendering of punitive or exemplary damages, the courts have generally held that since the damages are awarded to punish the wrongdoer, it would be contrary to the best interest of the public if that punishment were paid by the insurance company. See Exemplary Damages. See Extra Contractual Damages. See Intentional Acts. See Punitive Damages.

Punitive Damages: Damages awarded over and above the judgment to the plaintiff for the actual loss, and assessed as a punishment to the defendant for egregious conduct such as fraud, malice, or wanton conduct. See Exemplary Damages. See Extra Contractual Damages. See Intentional Acts. See Public Policy.

Pure Comparative Negligence. See Comparative Negligence.

Pure Loss Ratio: The percentage of the insurance premium allocated to pay only the loss, without consideration for the loss expense payments. See Combined Loss Ratio. See Loss Ratio.

Q

Quantum Merit: An issue in equity that states that the degree of liability (usually under a contract matter) should be determined by the reasonableness of the actions called for under said contract, and that no party should be unjustly enriched from such dealings.

Quid Pro Quo (Latin): The exchange of items of equal value between parties to a contract, or other business or legal dealings.

Quota Share Primary Coverage Participation: A program for providing, by more than one insurer, insurance or reinsurance coverage for a given risk or group of risks. The coverage, including losses, premiums and often expenses, is shared by the participating carriers on the basis of their individual participation, usually expressed as a percentage of the entire covered amount. Unlike excess insurance written over a primary policy, quota share participants providing primary insurance coverage generally responds to losses on a "first dollar" basis, with each participant paying their proportionate share. See Quota Share Reinsurance. See Excess Insurance.

Quota Share Reinsurance Coverage: In reinsurance written on a quota share basis, the reinsurers contribute above the cedant's retention on the basis of their individual percentage, rather than on specific layers as is the case with "stop loss" or catastrophe reinsurance coverage. See Stop Loss/Catastrophe Reinsurance. See Quota Share Primary Insurance.

Quote: The colloquial term meaning to provide a written or verbal offer of the amount needed to pay for insurance protection. See Premium.

R

Real Party in Interest: The person or entity with the legal right to make a claim and/or bring a lawsuit on any given matter.

Reasonable Doubt: In criminal litigation, the judge and jury must consider all evidence presented by all parties, and determine if the guilt of the person charged could be determined beyond a doubt that is reasonable. See Preponderance of the Evidence.

Reciprocal Insurance Company: A group or association of people or entities cooperating, usually through an attorney-in-fact, for the purpose of insuring themselves and each other. See Captive Company. See Interinsurance Exchange. See Mutual Company. Stock Company.

Recusal: The process whereby a judge voluntarily agrees to not hear a matter that would otherwise be before him, or is disqualified by some higher authority from hearing said matter.

Red-Lining: The action of predetermining that a person or entity is unacceptable as an insured, based on non-insurance related criteria such as race, origin, location of domicile, or other such subjective considerations. See Blacklisting.

Reformation: The act of rewriting a contract to change original mistakes to that written instrument, and make it properly reflect the original agreement between the parties to that contract. See Policy Reformation. See Rescission.

Rehabilitation: The act of returning a person who has been injured to their previous physical and/or mental state before injury, or to return them to a condition as close thereto as is medically possible. Rehabilitation may be medical, physical, psychological, vocational, or, in some cases may refer to real property.

Reinsurance: The practice of the transfer of all, or a part, of one or many risks between the original insurer(s) that wrote the insurance and the reinsurer(s) who agree to share the premium and losses. See Assumed Reinsurance. See Ceded Reinsurance.

Release of Liability Form: A document that agrees to finalize the claim between parties by acknowledging certain conditions and forever discharges the party being released from any future claims from the same incident. See Covenant Not to Sue. See General Release.

Remand: The act of the appellate court in sending a matter back to the court from which it came, in order to have one or several matters readdressed for further action. With a remand, no action is taken by the appellate court to confirm or overturn the underlying court's decision on matters such as liability, damages, etc. See Appeal.

Remittitur: A decrease by the trial court judge in the amount of an award or verdict rendered by a jury. See Additur.

Rent: As a noun, an agreement (written or oral) between the owner of certain property (the "lessor") and one or more people (the "lessee") who wish to have or use the property for a definite or indeterminate period of time. The lessee will generally pay the lessor an agreed fee (usually periodically, and referred to as "rent") for said use. See Lease.

As a verb, "to rent" would be the act of acquiring (by the lessee) and/or conveying (by the lessor) temporary possession of property for a specific purpose such as housing, business use, etc.

Repetitive Trauma: An injury occurring as a result of a continuous type of activity, which by itself as a single incident would not normally cause harm or injury. It is the repetitive nature of the activity, rather than the activity itself, which does the damage. See Cumulative Trauma.

Replacement Cost: The value of an item based on the cost to replace it with like kind and quality at current prices without deduction for depreciation, betterment or usage. See Actual Cash Value.

Replevin: A legal action in which the rightful owner of goods takes those goods back from a person or entity that wrongfully possesses them.

Rescission: The unmaking of a contract from its inception, as if it had never existed, which differs from the termination of a contract that merely ceases all terms as of the date of said termination. See Reformation.

Reservation of Rights: The activity of a party stating unilaterally that the actions taken by that party shall not constitute a waiver of any of the party's rights. Also, the document expressing such unilateral proclamation. See Non-Waiver Agreement.

Reserves: The amount of money set aside by the insurance company to pay for known and/or unknown claims, and associated costs. See Case Reserves. See Expense Reserves. See I.B.N.R. See Loss Reserve.

Res ipsa loquitur (Latin): The Thing Speaks for Itself. A rebuttable presumption that an instrument causing damage was in the exclusive control of the defendant, and the injury would not have normally occurred in the absence of negligence.

Res judicata (Latin): The matter has already been settled by the courts. This precludes a legal action wherein the issues and parties are the same as in a previously resolved legal matter.

Respondent: The person or entity against whom an injured worker, in a Workers' Compensation matter, files a claim with the appropriate State or Federal agency having jurisdiction for such matters. See Claimant. See Applicant.

Respondeat superior (Latin): The legal principle that the master is responsible for the acts of his servant, and the principal is accountable for the acts of his agent. See Agency.

Retention Amount: That amount of a claim that the insured agrees they will pay before the coverage provider becomes involved with the loss. In primary coverage, this acts as a deductible. In reinsurance, this acts as a level that the cedant will bear on their own, without reinsurance participation.

Retro Active Coverage: Insurance protection that is granted to the insured by the insurer, after an act or incident has already occurred.

Retrocessional Reinsurance: Reinsurance provided by one reinsurance company to another reinsurer. This is reinsurance of reinsurance. See Retrocessionaire.

Retrocessionnaire: The party or entity that accepts reinsurance coverage on business of another reinsurer. Also known as the assuming reinsurer. See Assuming Reinsurer. See Ceding Reinsurer. See Retrocessional Reinsurance.

Retro-premium: An insurance premium, which is calculated at the end of the policy period rather than before the policy's inception. This allows the insurer to capture the amount of the losses paid for by the insurer, and still provide for a profit to the insurer. See Earned Premium. See Gross Premium. See Net Premium. See Premium. See Written Premium.

Return Premium: The amount of the insurance premium that is due to be returned to the insured when the policy lapses, or is cancelled.

RICO: The Organized Crime Control Act of 1970 (commonly referred to as "Racketeer Influenced and Corrupt Organization" act). A federal statute aimed at prosecuting individuals and/or businesses whose activities have ties to organized crime.

Rider: An attachment to an insurance policy that changes or modifies the language, terms, or conditions in the policy itself. See Endorsement.

Risk: That which causes or increases the possibility of a loss, or potential loss. See Hazard. See Peril.

Risk Manager: The person who is responsible for overseeing the insurance requirements of a company.

Risk Rating: The action by underwriters of grouping similar types of exposures so as to consider them as one of a group, rather than each individually.

S

Salvage: After a loss, damaged property that has been restored, or that portion of said property that was not damaged.

Satisfaction of Judgment: A document filed with the court indicating that the judgment rendered in a particular case has now been satisfied by the party or parties against whom the judgment was rendered. See Judgment.

Save Harmless Agreement: A contract clause whereby one party agrees to assume the liability of another. See Hold Harmless Clause. See Indemnification Agreement.

Scope of Employment: In Workers' Compensation, the injury must be incurred "in the scope of the employment"; i.e., referring to the time, place and circumstances of the incident as relating to the nature, conditions, obligations and incidents of the employment. See Course of Employment. See Course and Scope of Employment. See Workers' Compensation.

Self Insurance: The act of setting aside funds to meet possible future losses, rather than insuring against those losses through the purchase of an insurance policy.

Self Insured Retention: That portion of a loss that the insured agrees to bear on his own, without indemnification from the insurer. Unlike a deductible, the insurer will generally not adjust the loss or otherwise be involved if the loss is valued within the retention amount. See Deductible.

Sequester: The act of isolating the jury to insure they do not become involved with material that may be relative to the case on which they are sitting, but which has not been properly introduced as evidence at the trial.

Serving a Complaint/ Service of Process: The act of presenting the defendant(s) in a lawsuit with a copy of the complaint as filed with the court, setting forth the allegations of the plaintiff, and demanding the defendant appear to answer those charges. See Filing Complaint. See Long Arm Statute.

Settlement: The act of resolving a dispute between two or more parties.

Severability of Interest Clause: A clause found in most liability insurance contracts that indicates that the various parties who may be insured under the policy will each be treated separately. See Policy Conditions.

Several Liability: Legal responsibility of a person or entity, without the requirement of another entity being also held accountable. In court proceedings, there is no requirement that a joinder of another party be used. See Joint Liability.

Short Rate Cancellation: The cost assessed by an insurance company when a policy is canceled by the insured prior to the expiration date, and which generally is greater than the proportionate share of the premium for the remaining time left on the policy. See Cancellation. See Policy Cancellation.

Sight Draft: Similar to a check in that it is issued to another for payment, but is not payable until the maker authorizes the bank to release the funds necessary to honor the instrument. See Draft.

Slander: The uttering, orally, of false and defamatory statements concerning another. See Libel.

Special Damages: The actual and measurable damages sustained.

Standard of Care: Care which a reasonably prudent person would exercise under like or similar circumstances. The standard may differ for matters arising out of, or related to, property, depending on the status of the injured party; i.e., visitor, licensee, trespasser, etc. The standard in automobile incidents may also be greater as it relates to drivers for hire and for those charging for transportation. See Negligence.

Statute: A law enacted by a legislative body, as opposed to that group of laws known as common law which emanate from court findings and judgments. See Common Law. See Statutory Law.

Statute of Limitations: The time period after an incident in which a legal action must be brought, or be barred forever. See Laches.

Statutory Law: The laws that have been enacted by various legislative bodies and on which the courts rely for decisions pertaining to the various subjects involved. See Common Law. See Equity. See Statute.

Stay: A court's action of stopping, temporarily, a judicial proceeding.

Stipulation: An agreement to accept certain matters in court proceedings, rather than insist that they be tried or that their validity be based on evidence submitted.

Stock Insurance Company: A company owned by investors who purchase shares of stock in the company, and who may or may not be insured with the company. The value of the shares of stock and any possible dividends are derived from the financial worth and profitability of the company. See Captive Company. See Mutual Company. See Reciprocal Company.

Stop Loss/Catastrophe Reinsurance: The method for providing reinsurance to ceding companies on the basis of specific dollar amounts, layered above the retention amount that is maintained by the ceding carrier. Each participating Stop Loss Reinsurer becomes involved with the payment of a loss when all other reinsurers participating below that reinsurer's layer have exhausted their amount of coverage. See Quota Share Reinsurance.

"Straw Man/Straw Party": A party who is put up in name only as part of a deal, but who has no real stake in the matter. Usually used to mask the identity of one or more of the true parties in interest to the matter.

Strict Liability: In products liability, the legal doctrine that states the manufacturer and/or seller of certain products, deemed to be inherently dangerous, looses some available defenses to actions arising from use of the product.

Subagent: A person appointed by someone who is himself an agent, or is acting in an agency relationship.An "assistant" agent. See Agent.

Subpoena: A summons issued by a court in a legal proceeding to appear before the court to give testimony and be examined in the matter at hand. See Subpoena Duces Tecum.

Subpoena duces tecum: A summons by a court in a legal proceeding for a person in possession of certain material to appear with the material for an examination of same. See Subpoena.

Subrogation: The substitution of one party in a claim for another, whereby the first party obtains the rights and claims of the second party. See Third Party Complaint. See Cross Complaint.

Sue and Labor Clause: A portion of many marine insurance policies that allows the insured to take some actions to attempt to mitigate a loss, without those actions being later considered to prejudice, and thereby jeopardize, the coverage in the policy. The clause is meant to encourage the insured to attempt to lessen the loss.

Summary Judgment: The granting of a motion for a verdict on behalf of any party to a lawsuit on the grounds that there is no material issue of fact, and that the petitioning party is entitled to prevail as a matter of law. See Directed Verdict. See Nonsuit.

Summons: A document which provides jurisdiction over a party to a lawsuit, and which calls the party to appear at a given time and place to be examined. See Notice to Appear.

Supervening Negligence: To be in effect (a) the injured party (plaintiff) must already be in a position of danger; (b) the offending party (defendant) must recognize that the party in danger is unable to avoid the emanate danger; (c) the offending party (plaintiff) must be able to save the person in danger from said danger; and (d) the offending party (defendant) does not take the steps necessary to save the party in danger. See Intervening Cause.

Surety Bond: A bond that obligates the guarantor to pay a third party if the party taking the bond fails to pay what is owed to the third party. See Appeal Bond. See Bond. See Fidelity Bond. See Performance Bond.

Surplus: The amount of assets the insurance company owns, less their liabilities. In most states, an insurer's surplus determines the amount of new business (added potential liability) the carrier can write. See Company Surplus. See Underwriting Surplus.

Surplus Lines: The insurance market that provides coverage when traditional or normally existing insurance markets are not available. Excess and Surplus Lines policies are usually acquired from "non-admitted" insurance carriers. See Admitted Insurance Company. See Excess and Surplus Lines Brokers. See Non-admitted Insurance Company.

T

"Tail" Coverage: Insurance protection purchased to cover the time following the cessation of coverage under a Claims Made Policy. See Prior Acts Coverage.

Temporary Disability: A benefit under Workers' Compensation laws that provides an injured worker, who is unable to continue employment for a temporary period of time due to compensable injuries sustained, with some portion of his wages while in this unemployable condition. See Permanent Disability. See Workers' Compensation.

Third Party: In insurance matters, the party, other than the insured, who will benefit from the coverage provided by the insurance, such as a liability claimant seeking damages from the insured. See First Party.

Third Party Administrator: A person or entity that agrees to handle, for a fee, the claims and/or other business aspects of an insurance company or self-insured group.

Third Party Beneficiary: Although not a party to a contract or agreement, a person who, by their position or standing, derives benefit from the agreement or contract of other parties. See Beneficiary. See Third Party.

Third Party Complaint: A pleading, filed by a defendant in a lawsuit, in order to include some other entity, not a party to the original suit. This is unlike a Cross Complaint that alleges the defendant has a claim against the plaintiff in the original matter before the court. See Cross Complaint.

Third Party Defendant: The person being brought into an existing lawsuit by a defendant to that lawsuit, claiming the party bringing the charges has a claim against the Third Party Defendant in the same matter as is before the court in the original action.

Tort: A civil wrong. A legal action arising out of a breach of a duty by one party to another. See Duty. See Liability. See Negligence.

Tort Feasor: A wrongdoer; one who commits a tort or civil wrong. See Joint Tort Feasor.

Treaty Reinsurance: An agreement between a cedant and a reinsurer that the reinsurer will provide reinsurance coverage on all policies written by the ceding company for a particular type of primary coverage. The reinsured amounts, premium sharing, and other particulars are often set forth in the treaty agreement and do not require a specific submission and acceptance for the reinsurance coverage to be placed. See Facultative Reinsurance.

Trial: The judicial examination of facts in question between parties, and the rendering of a decision on the issues. See Arbitration. See Mediation.

U

Umbrella Policy: A type of excess insurance policy that generally provides coverage above the amounts found in other specified policies, or groups of policies, owned by the same insured. It is often used colloquially to infer a type of excess policy that provides coverage to a greater number of policies than a regular excess policy. See Excess Insurance.

Unallocated Loss Adjustment Expense (U.L.A.E): Costs incurred by the claims handling facility that cannot be related, and therefore allocated, to a specific claim file. These include such items as claims employees' salaries, office supplies, rent, utilities, etc. See Allocated Loss Adjustment Expenses (ALAE).

Under-insured: That condition which exists when the amount of insurance on a particular piece of property is less than the property is worth, or less than the agreed amount of coverage to be carried. This may be inadvertent, or may be done on purpose with the idea of reducing the amount of premium. See Over-insured.

Under Insured Motorist Coverage: Similar to Uninsured Motorist Coverage, except this insurance will come into effect if the policyholder (or other insured under the policy) has an accident with another motorist who has less than the limits prescribed in this coverage. The policyholder's insurance company will, in effect, supplement the other driver's coverage for the insured's benefit. See Uninsured Motorist Coverage.

Underwriter: The insurance company employee, or other party assuming the risk, who will determine if the risk and premium are consistent enough so as to approve and issue a contract of insurance.

Underwriting File: The records and material accumulated by the underwriter in investigating the risk prior to issuing a policy, and maintaining contact with the risk as the policy is in effect.

Underwriting Intent: What was meant to be covered by, and/or excluded from, a particular policy when it was written. This may differs from the literal and specific wording in the policy contract. If all parties agree and/or if there is incontrovertible proof of such intent, this may be binding and take precedent over the policy wording.

Underwriting Surplus: The amount of assets the insurance company owns, less their liabilities. In most states, an insurer's surplus determines the amount of new business (added potential liability) the carrier can write. See Company Surplus. See Surplus.

Unearned Premium: The calculation of the ratio, or percentage, which the total amount of the premium charged for an insurance policy bears to the amount of time not yet lapsed on the policy. It is the premium for that portion of insurance coverage remaining to be provided during the time the policy has until expiration; i.e., the written premium, less the earned premium. See Earned Premium: See Written Premium.

Uniform Commercial Code: Drafted by the National Conference of Commissioners on Uniform State Laws, this governs all commercial transactions. It is accepted by all states except Louisiana.

Uninsurable Risk: A risk that cannot be calculated as to value, potential loss, etc., and is therefore unable to be insured. See Non-insurable Risk.

Uninsured Motorist Coverage: Insurance coverage, usually voluntarily purchased, to supplement automobile liability coverage. This insurance protects the policyholder from losses incurred if said policyholder (or other insured) is injured or damaged by a motorist who is uninsured. The policyholder's insurance company stands in the shoes of the uninsured motorist as if that uninsured motorist was insured. See Under Insured Motorist Coverage.

Unjust Enrichment: The legal doctrine which indicates one party should not be permitted to be enriched at the expense of another, and should make proper restitution of property or benefits if obtained inappropriately or by means not equitable to the other party.

V

Venue: The geographical location in which the court has authority over a matter, and is therefore empowered to hear the case. See Jurisdiction.

Verdict: The final decision of the judge or jury in a lawsuit, after considering evidence and hearing testimony.

Verdict N.O.V: A court entered judgment in favor of one of the parties to a lawsuit, even though the jury has already entered a judgment in favor of the other party. This overturns the jury verdict. See N.O.V.

Vexatious: Having no reasonable or probable excuse.

Voir dire (Latin) (To speak the truth.): The preliminary examination of witnesses or jurors by the court as to their suitability to act as said witness or juror in the case before the court.

Volunteer: One who acts or provides a service without a legal responsibility to do so. The degree of duty owed to a volunteer may vary in determining the liability of another party. See Liability. See Negligence.

W

Waiver: The voluntary or intentional giving up of a known right. Often used in concert with, but differing from, the term "estoppel". See Estoppel.

Wanton Act: An action or conduct done in reckless disregard of the consequences, and without concern for the possible damage to others that the act may cause. Such acts are more egregious than negligence or gross negligence. See Willful Act.

Willful Act: An action or conduct done in reckless disregard of the consequences, and without concern for the possible damage to others that the act may cause. Such acts are more egregious than negligence or gross negligence. See Wanton Act.

Workers' Compensation Coverage: A type of insurance protection purchased by employers to provide payment for medical attention, lost wages and disability resulting from injuries to their employees who are hurt during the course and scope of their employment. Specific state law in the jurisdiction in which the employer is doing business and/or where the injured worker lives, works, or was hired usually mandates the provisions and requirements for this type insurance. See Longshoremen's and Harbor Workers' Act.

Writ: A written order by the court to command that something be done, or that something not be done, and generally directed at one or more specific individuals.

Writ of Certiorari: An order from a higher court to a lower court indicating whether the higher court will hear an issue or case referred to it. See Certiorari.

Written Premium: The total amount of the premium charged, when a policy is issued, for the insurance coverage from inception to expiration. See Earned Premium. See Unearned Premium. See Gross Premium. See Net Premium. See Retro-Premium.

X

"X-Mod": In Workers' Compensation premium calculations, the modification or adjustment of the basic (or general class) premium, to reflect an increase or decrease in that basic premium, due to a higher or lower than expected frequency and/or severity of claims. See Exposure Modifier.

Index

Voir Dire, 56, 193

W

"Wall of Silence", 12
Workers' Compensation, 9, 35, 61-63,
        78, 89-90, 101-102, 108-121, 123,
        143, 146, 151-152, 158-159, 161, 169-
        170, 174, 176, 184-186, 189, 193-194
Workers Compensation Policy, 90, 109,
        111, 120-121, 123
Writ of Certiorari, 62, 148, 194
Written Premium, 69-70, 156, 161, 178,
        185, 192, 194

X

"X" Mod, 111, 159

Y

Yangtze River, 4

NOTES

NOTES